TOMORROW IS OUR
PERMANENT ADDRESS

This volume is part of a series of books published by Harper &
Row, Publishers, Inc., for the Lindisfarne Association. The
series is under the general editorship of William Irwin
Thompson and is devoted to an exploration of the newly
emerging planetary culture and the future evolution of humanity.

Other books in the Lindisfarne series:
Passages about Earth: An Exploration of the New Planetary Culture, by
 William Irwin Thompson
Sri Aurobindo, or the Adventure of Consciousness, by Satprem
*The Findhorn Garden: Pioneering a New Vision of Man and Nature in
 Cooperation,* by the members of the Findhorn Community
*Earth's Answer: Explorations of Planetary Culture at the Lindisfarne
 Conferences,* eds. Michael Katz, William Parker Marsh, and
 Gail Gordon Thompson

TOMORROW IS OUR PERMANENT ADDRESS

The Search for an Ecological Science of

Design as Embodied in the Bioshelter

JOHN TODD
NANCY JACK TODD

PHOTOGRAPHS BY JOHN TODD

DRAWINGS BY SOLSEARCH ARCHITECTURE
Cambridge, U.S.A., and Charlottetown, Canada

A Lindisfarne Book

HARPER & ROW, PUBLISHERS

New York

Cambridge   London
Hagerstown   Mexico City
Philadelphia   São Paulo
San Francisco   Sydney

1817

FIRST EDITION

Designer: *Janice Stern*

Library of Congress Cataloging in Publication Data

Todd, John.
    Tomorrow is our permanent address.

    "A Lindisfarne book."
    1. Dwellings—Environmental engineering.   2. Ecology.
I. Todd, Nancy, joint author.   II. Title.
TH4812.T62 1979   728.6   78-2171
ISBN 0-06-014319-3
ISBN 0-06-090712-6 pbk.

80 81 82 83 10 9 8 7 6 5 4 3 2 1

This book is dedicated to all New Alchemists, both once and future, whose commitment is the real alchemy and without whose work the Arks never would have been.

We also wish to acknowledge the invaluable contribution of Solsearch, whose integration of architecture with our biological design was the critical element.

Contents

Foreword

BY WILLIAM IRWIN THOMPSON

The Miniaturization of History

A bioshelter is a miniaturization of an ecosystem. It seems fitting, therefore, that my introduction to a book about bioshelters should be about miniaturization *through* history in an essay that is itself a miniaturization *of* history.

Because we are living in a period of cultural transformation, we are highly conscious of the cultural transformations that have come before. Seeing where we have been helps us to sense where we are going; but, of course, past and future are simply the mysterious dimensions of the present: the image we see in our rearview mirror is totally determined by our moving position in the present. So when a cultural historian like myself looks into the rearview mirror and writes "history," he is really writing a description of the present.

When I look at history, I see six great cultural transformations: the Hominization of the Primates in the Pliocene, Symbolization and the origins of notation and art in the Upper Paleolithic, Agriculturalization in 9000 B.C., Civilization in 3500 B.C., Industrialization in the eighteenth century A.D., and, finally, the cultural transformation we are now living in, the Planetization of Humanity.

9

The first transformation, the Hominization of the Primates, should really be called the feminization of the primates, because it all started when we were kicked out of the forest in the Pliocene. We became so frightened, being out in the open and subject to predation, that the females unconsciously lured the males around them by abandoning the old estrus system to become open to sexuality at all times. Lured by the power of pheromones, the males left off palling around with their buddies in the old male pair-bonding system and clustered around the females. Next thing you know, there is a whole new setup, with the males scrounging and bringing the food back to a home base, and the females gathering with the infants clinging tightly to their hair, as tightly as the females clung to the protection of the clump of trees in the open savanna. And with all of that, the basic divisions of labor between the sexes was established.

So, the origins of human culture come from the female. Women did it again in the next big change, Symbolization. When language began to emerge, it split consciousness by creating the unconscious and the conscious. Like an island rising out of the sea, language was a piece of the old ocean floor held up to new light, and the symbol, like a piece of coral or a rock, could help to relate the one to the other. One seemingly small thing that helped relate the one to the other was menstruation, for it established the first observable periodicities between the phases of the moon and the internal life of the womb, with ovulation at the full, and menstruation at the dark of the moon. In observing the synchronicity between their bodies and nature, and in keeping track of the ten lunar months of pregnancy on the lunar tally sticks of the midwife, woman was the first to establish the system of notation and symbolism upon which all later calendrical systems are based. So the roots of science, *contra* Alexander Marshack, are with women; it's the story of the Great Mother holding up the lunar calendar incised on the crescent of the bison's horn (the well-known Venus of Laussel), and not the story of the Great Father with his phallic *baton de commandement*.

The third basic change came again from women when, through gathering wild cereals, they discovered that they could collect more food than man the hunter could ever kill. But since the food required storage bins and heavy grinding stones, they began to settle down to create agriculture and the Neolithic village. Unfortunately, agriculture gave us enough of a surplus that men had some time on their hands. Since they now had "property" that could be taken away, the men found that trading and raiding could be as exciting as the old days of the hunt, and so warfare came into being.

After the domestication of plants and animals in Agriculturalization came the next big change, the domestication of women, or Civilization. Warfare enabled the old custom-bound, religious, matrilineal society of the Neolithic village to grow into the great city with its patriarchal structure, its great male gods, its military walls, its religiously controlled economic surplus, and its permanent armies. Small wonder that the Sumerian goddess Inanna comes to the great male god Enki and says: "I, the woman, why did you treat differently; where are my prerogatives."

Enki responds by saying: "Enki perfected greatly that which was woman's task." A woman as a cook is a mere housewife, but a man is a chef. Woman may have invented the lunar tally stick, but man takes it over to create writing, the measurement of wealth in the temple storehouse. But in the early days of Civilization they were not that far removed from the Neolithic era of the Great Goddess, and so a certain balancing between the sexes is still affirmed. The storehouse is the womb, the cornucopia; the grain stored in it, the male seed. The writing stylus is the phallus, but the image pressed upon the soft, submissive clay is the ancient Paleolithic sign of life, the vulva, the pubic triangle.

From 3500 B.C. to the eighteenth century A.D., all the civilizations of the world are agricultural, but then in Great Britain another big change comes along, and we see the next transformation, Industrialization. Industrialization is really an intensification of Civilization, and so through science and technology the culture becomes even more patriarchal and militaristic than its Sumerian ancestor.

In Hominization, the old forest home had been absorbed into the clump of trees, the new home base for the protohominids. In Symbolization the animals were absorbed into the artistic images on bones and cave walls. In Agriculturalization the plants were absorbed, and in Civilization women were absorbed. In each case of cultural absorption there was an attendant process of miniaturization: first the forest had been miniaturized in the clump of trees in the home base; then the animals had been miniaturized in an image or a lunar tally stick; then plants were miniaturized in a garden; and finally women and Neolithic matrilineal culture were miniaturized in the patriarchal household. In the Industrial Revolution all nature was surrounded and miniaturized by culture. The wrought-iron and glass structure of the Great Exhibition of 1851 surrounded the trees and fountains of London's Hyde Park and proclaimed for all the world to see that in the Crystal Palace of industrial technology, wild nature had been turned into a potted plant. (Small wonder that most Victorian drawing rooms became civilized jungles of potted ferns.) We historians now see all this, of course, with 20/20 hindsight. Then people thought they were *returning* to nature in romanticism, and the Great Exhibition featured such camouflage of Industrialization as Sherwood Forest Robin Hood chairs, Gothic sewing scissors, and rose-decorated sewing machines. Through the Medieval Court in the Crystal Palace, everyone grooved on nostalgia and admired the cute little vines engraved on the legs of the machines. You can see it all in the world's first *Whole Earth Catalogue,* the catalogue for the Great Exhibition itself.

What was true of Industrialization is true of Planetization. A nostalgic and false consciousness is trying to camouflage the structure with a romantic content. All the artifacts and cultures of the world were miniaturized in Stewart Brand's *Whole Earth Catalogue,* and although people grooved on wood stoves in fantasies of self-sufficiency, the catalogue was absorbing everything into itself. (All culture was being absorbed and miniaturized as the preparation for stuffing it into one of Gerard O'Neill's proposed space colonies.)

But Stewart Brand, Gerard O'Neill, or even Herman Kahn do not express the full dimensions of Planetization. In what Sri Aurobindo would call "the Descent of the Supra-mental," there is a new level of human consciousness that is now surrounding, absorbing, and miniaturizing the old civilized and technological consciousness. The civilizational process of individuation, of separating *man* from nature, is now finishing; the instinctive, collective unconscious that had been pushed down by civilization, and therefore kept exploding up in nativistic movements all during the five-thousand-year period of Civilization has now been reabsorbed. A mythopoeic way to describe this event would be to call it the reconciliation of Adam with his first wife, Lilith. Nature and the feminine no longer threaten us as a Great Mother pulling back the individuated consciousness into her dark earth. Now mankind seeks a wife and not a mother or a concubine. Now *man*kind becomes humanity in achieving a species level of consciousness. The event has been predicted for some time, by prophets from Jesus to Whitman, but whether we speak of "the Mystical Body of Christ," or Messiah, Mahdi, or Maitreya, all the religions of our world know about this transformation in which humanity realizes that it is a single being. Now as we move up to a species level of consciousness in harmony with the biosphere, the field of ecology becomes a description of spiritual processes; it becomes for us what alchemy was for the Renaissance initiate. When now we speak about the harmony of consciousness with the biosphere, of the relationship of science to Gaia, we merely speak in a modern idiom for what others knew as the Alchemical Wedding of Christ and his Church. The search for the appropriate vessel, the quest for the Holy Grail, is finished when we realize that nothing less than the entire planet can be the appropriate cup for the transformation of matter into food, and food into flesh.

As this planetary realization of a New Alchemy comes over us, we also see a complementary process of miniaturization moving along with it. The universe becomes miniaturized in the individual; the fully individuated being becomes the cosmic holograph. No longer need the ego, broken off from nature and alienated from itself, be compressed into the mass of the state. When, in the mystical vision of Nicholas of Cusa, "the Center is everywhere and the circumference nowhere," the need for a centralized, authoritarian government is transcended. Of course, all our old governments are not prepared for these Whitmanesque prophecies of "Democratic Vistas," and so the latter days of Civilization will be a cracking of the hard casing to release the seed. Since we all live in a business civilization, the first cracking up will come in the world economy. Idols will topple as we realize that we have invested consciousness into a mere dead thing; since the $ is the central idol of the econometric state, the dollar sign will fall on its side and the bars that cross it will melt and turn it into a sign for infinity.

It is not by accident that the ecology of John and Nancy Todd is called New Alchemy and that the bioshelters of their design are called Arks. Whether these become arks of new covenants with nature or arks of survival will depend on us, for in many ways the work of John and Nancy Todd expresses the political ambiguities of our transitional age. On the one hand, they are strategies for decentralization, enabling families to live with high culture in wilderness circumstances; on the other hand, they are the miniaturization of ecosystems NASA needs for the design of space colonies. When the managers of the econometric state look at the miniaturization of ecosystems, they do not think of E. F. Schumacher's book, *Small Is Beautiful,* or Gary Snyder's phrase, "To live lightly on the earth"; they see computer chips and bioshelters as new ways *man* can keep his dominion over the machine he calls "spaceship earth."

The polarization is not sharp now, and most people cannot tell the difference between a Buckminster Fuller and a John Todd, a Howard Odum and a Gregory Bateson, partly because they are not yet on opposite sides of a political conflict. But things are coming to a new sharpness, and the logarithmic spiral of human history is tightening to a point in the mid-1980s. Then we shall have to choose sides in an archetypal battle between good and evil we have not seen since the days of Hitler. Then the choice between authoritarian, technocratic governments, supported by nuclear energy and capital-intensive economies of scale, and expressing themselves in the culture of urban growths like Calcutta, Rio, and New York, on the one hand, and on the other, the decentralization of cities, the Planetization of nations, and the transformation of consciousness, will be radiantly clear. But one thing is already certain, and that is that John and Nancy Todd are not the countercultural hippies on the farm that the proponents of nuclear energy take them to be; they are the real political scientists working in the heart of the cultural transformation of our time. What will become of them is what is going to happen to us.

William Irwin Thompson
Christmas Eve, 1978
Lindisfarne in Manhattan

tomorrow is our permanent address
and they'll scarcely find us (if they do
we'll move away still further: into now
e. e. cummings

PART I

The Historical Climate

A bioshelter is one actualization of an emerging theory of design that is based on natural systems, of a biotechnic approach to the problems of human sustenance. In its potential, it opens up horizons that could make a reality of Mr. Cummings's statement of faith in tomorrow being our permanent address. Yet because we create the future with our every decision and act in the present, and because the bioshelter is already a tangible, working reality, we include his closing couplet not in an elitist or escapist sense but in considering the promise it holds rather as an invitation, to "move away still further: into now."

The term *bioshelter* is one that has only recently come into usage. It was created by solar designers Sean Wellesley-Miller and Day Chahroudi, who were grappling for a name that would convey the connotations of a structure that at once contains biotic components and maintains a symbiotic relationship with its immediate exterior environment. It refers to a building housing a contained and miniaturized ecosystem. Relying on and responsive to the sun as its primary energy source, it is comparable to an organism in that it functions as a membrane between an inner and outer world, both living, whereas standard buildings are more like shells enclosing an artificial, static environment. A bioshelter is a growing structure in which such living components as microorganisms, vegetables, herbs, trees, fruits, flowers, insects, lizards, toads, and people interact to regulate the atmosphere, climate, and productivity of the whole.

The bioshelters discussed in this book are solar-heated facilities, one of which also contains living quarters for four people. The New Alchemy Institute has designed and built two such structures: one, the Cape Cod Ark at its center in Massachusetts; and the other, the Prince Edward Island Ark, on Prince Edward Island in Maritime Canada, which, as of 1978, is under the management of an indigenous island group, the Institute for Man and Resources. To date, both Arks are functioning more effectively than their initiators orginally had dared hope; sailing warmly through bitter winters, producing satisfying harvests of plants and fish, and at the same time maintaining their ecosystems in healthy equilibrium. As technology they represent innovations: in biological climate control, energy conservation, and intensive, indoor ecological cultivation of food. But these structures have a symbolic significance that far outweighs their technological accomplishments. As a tangible and practical working manifestation of systematic thought, the bioshelter gives rise to an image of the possibility for a changing relationship between modern or civilized humanity and the natural world. Unlike the future postulated by industrial society, whose likelihood of survival can be symbolized by the moments until midnight indicated by the hands on the clock of the *Bulletin of the Atomic Scientists,* such a possibility is, in the words of the cartoon character Pogo, confronted with insurmountable opportunities. The bioshelter is an early embodiment of the biological metaphor. Because it represents a new and very different paradigm for human sustenance, and a synthesis of science and technology with the living world, it is important that the reasons for its creation be as clearly understood as the structure itself.

There are almost as many theories about the origins of our present ecological crisis as there are about the fall of Rome. Most of them contain a certain grain of truth. But here the similarity ends, for the fate of Rome stands framed in time, but the events leading to our own crisis span the human relationship with the natural world from prehistory continuing to the present moment. Some would hold that it began with the dawn of agriculture, when our nomadic hunter-gatherer ancestors first conceived of the idea of selecting seeds, planting, harvesting, and then replanting them on the same piece of ground. Slowly, seasonal wanderings were replaced by a more settled existence. In time, established settlement patterns gave rise to previously unknown concepts of territory and property, and ultimately to the manipulation and exploitation of the natural world. Once established, the habit of exploitation proved so addictive that it was enlarged to subsume all forms of life, including human, and has thrived ever since.

With the beginnings of settlement and increased access to food through cultivation, the pressure for maintaining small, mobile groups, or tribes grew less. Greater numbers, in fact, became desirable to augment the labor potential of the group, ironically contributing both to the production and to the demand for food. It seems likely that this was when work as we know it was born. There is little question that hunter-gatherers maintained themselves with far less drudgery and fewer hours of toil than any other peoples. Population pressures eventually exacerbated the impulse to extend and control territory, and has provided us ever since with an unfailing source for disagreement and war.

There have been cultures that we call primitive— generally in a pejorative sense—that have evolved synergistically within an environment, maintaining themselves in comparatively stable numbers and in intimate rapport with their life-support base, so that their needs are met within the ongoing balance of the ecosystem. The Kalahari bush people, the Australian aborigine, the Tasaday, and other isolated and dwindling bands do so still, as did the native Americans of North America until the time of European settlement. But such cultures, like the natural landscape, have been encroached upon and virtually eliminated by those tribes, nations, and empires impelled by reasons political, economic, or religious that have interacted with the world around them in such a way as to contribute incrementally, over history, to our present state of ecological degeneration. The Judeo-Christian tradition has been much maligned for the failure of stewardship— in the Western world, at least—because of the alienation inherent in the concept that God "let men [sic] have dominion over the fish of the sea and over the fowl of the air, and over the cattle and over all the earth, and over every creeping thing that creepeth upon the earth." Yet much of the Mediterranean world had been deforested, much of Greece laid bare, and the cedars of Lebanon felled without assistance from ancient Jews or early Christians. The barrenness of the lands surrounding the

Mediterranean dates back to the pressures of ancient empires—quite literally, to the cradle of civilization. Although governments, religions, and economic systems have varied enormously in the degree and rate at which they have made inroads on the natural world—even where gentler religions like Buddhism and Hinduism are predominant—sheer numbers of people have drained an area of its diversity of biological species beyond its capacity to restore itself.

In spite of the tendency on the part of many human cultures to impinge unfavorably on their natural surroundings, it was not until the Age of Enlightenment that the intellectual foundations were laid for the scale of the present massive global onslaught. At that time, as scholars began to rediscover ancient knowledge, they became particularly absorbed with astronomy and, with their newly devised telescopes, turned their attention skyward and observed the movements of the stars. Galileo, in realizing that the earth was not, after all, the center of the universe, traumatically changed the human sense of its place in the cosmos. The discoveries of Galileo, Kepler, and their contemporaries opened the way for the eventual circumnavigation of the globe, the Age of Exploration, and the gradual extension of the hegemony of European culture to all the continents of the world. The philosophic implications of this period were far-reaching and determinative, for with the brilliant and rapid expansion of knowledge, concentrating its attention outward to the unexplored areas of the world and upward to the skies, the dazzled human mind was drawn ever farther from its grounding in the equally mysterious organic reality of its home planet. What Lewis Mumford has called the mechanocentric concept of the universe has dominated Western science and thought ever since, and is witnessed in our own fascination with the space program and with entertainment involving adventures in space. From the Renaissance on, that which could be measured, quantified, charted, and ultimately objectified or manipulated has been accepted as being real and worthy of study. Descartes further fostered the polarity between organic and intellectual life by dismissing knowledge that could not be demonstrated or corroborated intellectually, and we remain victims of this duality. What could not be known absolutely—forests or watersheds, whales or human beings—tended to be set aside and accordingly objectified. The principle of transcendence came into its own.

The explosion of knowledge from this period provided the fundamentals for a more all-encompassing science, far surpassing any that had been known previously. The same science bred the technology that has changed the surface of the earth. The beginnings of industrialism brought the widespread, imaginative, and efficient application of technology to human purposes. We have been enlarging on the tools and methods ever since.

There can be little question that the benefits of science and technology have been many, if unevenly distributed. We have gained in terms of knowledge, medicine, sanitation, industry, weaponry, and the entire technological backup that makes the standard of living of developed countries possible for them, and eagerly sought after by those less developed. Yet in spite of the advances and amenities their work has brought us, at the present, over half of the research scientists of the world are employed in military research and development, and a significant proportion of this research is used in developing the technology of mass destruction and repression. Beyond the threat of global extinction, it is also undeniable that the air masses hang pale brown over vast reaches of continents, that the forests remaining to us are rapidly dwindling, that deserts are spreading, and that many of the world's people live still in poverty and hunger. Hovering on the horizon of the future hang the twin shadows of nuclear holocaust and ecological catastrophe. Neither of these would threaten us without the science and technology we have created. Whatever the advantages we have reaped, the price has been high.

And yet a widely accepted facet of human psychology is the high level of altruistic and cooperative behavior that can occur in times of crisis. Our checkered history is as dotted with gestures of nobility, courage, and kindness as it is with pettiness and violence. One can entertain the hope that our present dilemma may yet spark within us a renewed awareness of the sacredness, fragility, and uniqueness of the life on this planet juxtaposed against the vastness of the cosmos, and of ourselves as inseparably and irrevocably part of that life. Such a change of consciousness postulates a change in the human relation to the natural world, a change from a mechanistic to an organic world view. To implement it would require a different kind of science and technology—one of life. Embryonic and tentative still, this science and technology are being born.

Although mystics and poets, naturalists, shamans, and philosophers have long despaired at the inroads being made on the natural world, as the threat continues unabated, the chorus of protest begins to swell concomitantly.

In the United States, the Vietnam War was the catalyst that accelerated criticism of a society rarely questioned. In protesting the war and the killing of a remote people, many Americans were brought to the realization that an economy based on ongoing growth and consumption was predicated on the continuous exploitation of resources—somewhere—that was imperialism whether it was called that or not. When and where this connection was made, the concept of environmentalism, whose proponents had for years been decrying the destruction of natural habitats, was raised to the level of ecology—to the beginnings of an understanding of the interconnectedness of politics and economics, of all human activities and the health of the natural environment, local, national, and world.

Once the clay foundation on which our society is structured had become apparent to a few people, the cracks in it became more readily discernible, and what began as a protest specifically against the war in Vietnam expanded into a more profound and radical critique. The generally youthful counterculture channeled its rejection of war and racism into a pragmatic search for alternative ways of supporting themselves that were closer to nature, less attached to the umbilical cord of consumer economics, and that employed simpler, less destructive technologies.

As the sixties continued, the feminist movement, which had been largely quiescent since achieving suffrage for women in 1919, reemerged as an embattled voice that insisted on being heard. The outrage over the war forced many women to confront the reality of their ineffectuality in the realm of public life. A vote was inadequate protection for the lives of one's sons, of American young men, and of the Vietnamese men, women, and children who suffered and died daily. It was becoming increasingly evident to many women, as it was to many men, that the control of society—and, indirectly, of their lives—lay beyond the vote, even beyond the exclusive province of government, in the interlocking directorates of what was coming to be called the military-industrial complex.

For many of those who joined the antiwar movement, criticism died with the end of the war. But for others, the seeds of doubt had developed into shoots too strong to ignore and to allow them to resume life as though nothing had happened. In the case of feminist thought, the struggle to protect life had at least two logical extensions. Faced with the indisputable reality of their powerlessness, some women extended their struggle for political influence to one for equality in a male-dominated society. The scales began to fall from the eyes of women as individuals and in groups, and they began to see the limitations of their position in the iron grip of patriarchal culture. The battles, both within themselves and with society, ensuing from that slow and still-dawning consciousness have taken and will take many forms. The connection between feminism and the ecology movement is well stated by the Jungian psychiatrist Irene Claremont de Castillejo,[1] who wrote: "The deeply buried feminine in us whose concern is the unbroken connection of all things is in passionate revolt against the stultifying, life-destroying anonymous machine of the civilization we have built."

Granted, not all or even most feminists would agree with this statement, but the greatest commonality between feminism and ecological thought lies in an underlying concern for life. Even as women demand equality with men in public and private life, they retain the biological bonding with life that has characterized their evolution. While this should not determine the personal destiny of the individual life, as feminist leaders have insistently and rightly declared, the female experience, in its rhythmic lunar cycles of ovulation and menstruation and, most often, childbearing and nursing, has always been more directly rooted in a broader biological experience than that of the male. This has given to women a more immediate sense of immanence in the natural world, a more direct knowledge of the stirrings of life-forces beyond sexual energies to the feminine than to the masculine reality. Rather, the contrasting trait that has proved to have survival value for men is the one that dominates the present world dynamic, that of transcendence.

The immanental quality that permeates a truly ecological perspective does not derive from feminism alone. Indirectly, of course, in reaction to demands that men carry their share of domestic life and care of children, feminism can claim credit for enhancing the nurturing side of men. But there have always been many men whose care for other forms of life has shown itself in gentle and enduring stewardship. It is this kind of concern that is being forced to battle with the dominant ethic of exploitation. Yet another wellspring of a more contemplative indwelling approach has come from the recent growth of Buddhist philosophy and practice in the West. In contrast to our more individualistic and fragmented traditions, the stillness of meditation and the teachings of the oneness or unity of life can engender a heightened appreciation of the immanental reality of the human place in the larger life.

Feminism, Eastern thought, political protest—these and

many others are among the strands that have led to the evolution of a movement that is at once critique and solution. Variously called alternative, appropriate, soft, renewable, nonviolent, and biotechnic technology, it is much more than technology. It is an approach, a way of thinking, and, for some, a way of life.

The deepest of its roots draw from far beyond the sixties, reaching back to the fierce independence of the North American homesteader, and further still, to the self-sufficient peasants and villagers of all cultures. But in modern society, in addition to the desire for some control over the forces of one's life, there is a dimension of deliberate rejection of the industrial machine. Among the earliest articulations of the present attempt to create an alternative to technological society was found in the pages of the *Whole Earth Catalogue,* which provided an exhaustive list of sources for both information and access to tools. The back-to-the-land homesteading movement that was well under way by the mid-sixties was finding its usually young practitioners often woefully lacking in both the intellectual and the physical tools for a life that had forsaken modern conveniences as the mediators between themselves and the natural world. The *Whole Earth Catalogue* was an eclectic compendium of literature, science, biology, cybernetics, folklore, and sixties funk, and was a pragmatic ency-clopedia of self-reliance at a time of a vacuum of such information, and, as such, a cornerstone of what it called "soft tech."

Another major influence, one who captured the imagi-nation of many people, was Buckminster Fuller. The bloom of geodesic domes in the late sixties, like plastic mushrooms after a rain, bear witness to his inspiration.

The first New Alchemy bioshelter, constructed in 1971, was such a dome. Yet it was Buckminster Fuller's conviction that applied intelligence and ingenuity could lead the way out of the modern impasse—that, and his wildly infectious enthusiasm and optimism—rather than any specific hardware or invention that gave early impetus to the search.

A quieter but equally pivotal figure was that of E. F. Schumacher. His book *Small Is Beautiful* was read internationally by homesteaders and government leaders, students, and business people. Its subtitle, "Economics As Though People Mattered," enlarged the either/or, communist/capitalist debate and spoke to an economics based on real, not industrial or created, needs. Dr. Schumacher introduced the idea of intermediate technology: a technology that falls somewhere between the most rudimentary tools that do little to relieve lives of backbreaking labor or drudgery, and the capital- and resource-demanding machinery with which we have bulldozed our landscape and created the industrial world. In the case of plowing, for example, he advocated machinery more complex and efficient than a stick to break the ground, but much smaller in size and impact than the giant machines that reduce the cultivation of food to monoculture and, ultimately, determine the course of production. In his writing and in his public lectures, by his nonthreatening, nonaccusatory approach, Dr. Schumacher helped to reduce the barrier between protagonists of the counterculture and the establishment.

Yet one of the most compelling and healthy aspects of the small but beautiful movement in which Drs. Fuller and Schumacher were instrumental is that its leaders or key figures are too numerous to list. In essence, it is a movement of all chiefs and no Indians in its decentralization, lack of hierarchy, disinterest in control and authority, and self-motivated involvement on the part of its participants. Whereas the dominant themes in world politics remain the arms trade, industrialization, development, and growth, there is a subculture made up of a growing and bonded network of like-minded fellow travelers who are trying to short-circuit the industrial structure, to live closer to the land, to consume less, to use less nonrenewable energy, and to exchange their wares and skills through trade, cooperatives, mutual aid, and an exchange of information that is not based on profit. There are such groups in far-flung places as Ethiopia, Tasmania, and Iran; Guatemala, India, and Swaziland; in every country in Europe; in New Zealand and Australia. Unlike the dominant world politics in which control is channeled through several enormously powerful nerve centers, the alternative is evolving a dynamic in which the periphery becomes the center, and the center is everywhere.

The many forces discussed above were and remain the matrix of New Alchemy. The Institute, as an entity, was formed in late 1969 in San Diego, California. At that time, several people from the group who were biologists had been doing research in what they came to call "doomwatch biology." One of their projects involved introducing minute amounts of DDT into the water of large tanks containing many species of fish. Knowing that the behavior of the fish in the tank was governed by the emission of chemical pheromones that facilitated olfactory communication and made a stable social hierarchy possible, they were curious as to the effects of the DDT. The result, as suspected, was nothing so outright as direct poisoning of the fish, but a jamming of the communication system and the behavior patterns on which the survival of the fish depended. This gradual erosion of subtle factors seemed, even then, a telling analogy of the unseen and little-known interconnections within the workings of an ecosystem.

At the same time we were receiving reports from other scientists of equally dismaying findings: of other damaging side effects from DDT, of nitrates from fertilizer runoff leaching into groundwater, of the buildup of mercury in the flesh of fish, of lead fallout in the air from automobile exhausts, to list only a few, and still overlooking the seepage of radioactive materials into the air, ground, and water. All reports pointed to similarly disturbing prophecies of exponential environmental deterioration. Wearying of engaging in an ongoing diatribe against the industrial and consumer system that had created and was fostering the problem, we began to ask ourselves a question that has since become the central paradigm of New Alchemy: Are there benign, ecologically viable alternatives to the present polluting, capital-intensive, and exploitative methods for sustaining human populations? Are there biological analogues for the industrial system? Or, as Robin Clarke put it, is it possible to have a technology that would be "valid for all people for all time"? The poet Gary Snyder's phrase "To live lightly on the earth" perhaps best captures the essence of the idea.

There was a second set of circumstances equally formative to the early thinking of New Alchemy. At that time, John Todd and Bill McLarney had been taking their biology classes from San Diego State on field trips to the dry, hilly country just north of the Mexican border.

Although the purpose of the excursions was the orthodox one of the study of plants and animals, there was a secondary motive. A group of friends had settled in the area, intending to homestead and wanting to do so as sensitively as possible. They applied to the collective biological expertise of our group. After our initial forays into the area, we were nonplussed to discover that, academic credentials notwithstanding, we had not the faintest idea of where to look for water, what to plant, or where to grow food. There were no native Americans remaining to ask.

Thrown back on our own resources, we determined to catalogue every detectable aspect of the life we observed there. Each person was assigned a category to research. Soil microbes, animals, plants, birds, rocks, insects, and worms were noted or collected, and studied. The work was as detailed and as thorough as possible within the constraints of the time allotted. After a matter of months, a few clues began to emerge. One was the discovery of a plant that required moisture at its roots, indicating the presence and location of water. A second find was a plant association that included miners' lettuce and was known to need good soil. With these resources we conceived of a design that would tap the water and lead it through a series of ponds. The possibility of a garden grew, and with it the prospects of a diet more extensive than manzanita berries. Students, faculty, and homesteaders buzzed with ideas: water collection and retention, a polyculture of fish and vegetables, chickens, ducks, rabbits, a goat, and the inevitable hot baths. Then, one morning, the landlady appeared and, due to the news that a proposed subdivision had been approved, increasing the value of the property, announced a raise in the rent. The bulldozers subsequently appeared on the rim of the hill, and the dream of our friends of coevolving with manzanita bushes and live oak ended. Yet our ill-fated adventure on the arid hills that we called the Ranch gave New Alchemy an invaluable perspective. We learned the folly of unconnected academic hubris and a respect for the inherent wisdom extant in even a barren-seeming bioregion. We learned that we were to be not only partners but junior partners in our subsequent relations with the natural world and that therein lay human survival.

In the summer of 1970 we left San Diego and crossed the country to settle on Cape Cod. With this move, what had begun as the tentative searchings of two creative and somewhat unorthodox biologists and a disheartened peacenik grew to a loosely knit, cooperative group, consisting of a handful of friends with fish tanks in their basements and experimental vegetable gardens in their yards. Most of us had full-time jobs, and New Alchemy was sandwiched into evenings and weekends. In 1972, with the first funding, we were able to rent an old dairy farm in a community called Hatchville. Since then, we have grown to an organization of salaried employees that still remains a company of friends. We are as many humanists as scientists, and all work, whether scientific research by PhDs, fund-raising, administration, or agricultural research and maintenance of the community gardens, is considered equally important. Everyone shares in domestic housekeeping and in lawn-mowing and general upkeep. All receive equal salaries, differentiated only by the number of hours we work each month. And when we run out of money, we run out together.

Funding is and always has been problematic, and until

1975 exclusively from private sources. The Ark on Prince Edward Island was funded by the Canadian federal government, and the land was donated by the provincial government of Prince Edward Island. The work on Cape Cod has been supported by private individuals and foundations. The greatest and most consistent help has come from a few individuals who share our vision and have been instrumental in its actualization. We also have a membership program that contributes considerably to our continuing survival. In 1977 we received a grant from the National Science Foundation to monitor and create mathematical models of the Cape Cod Ark.

The acquisition of the farm in Hatchville was a turning point for us, in that New Alchemy took on a physical as well as a theoretical reality and we were able, at last, to get properly started on our work.

Attempting to address the question of ecological alternatives in a tangible form, we concentrated our research on areas of basic human needs: those of food, energy, and shelter. We wanted to know whether it was possible to cultivate foods intensively while not destroying the life of the soil or of the surrounding area, and perhaps even to improve the soil and to restore biological diversity. Initially, we concentrated on organic vegetable gardening. More recently, we have begun a project directed toward a more permanent form of agriculture based on tree crops. In the gardens, our yields have increased annually as the composted, cultivated soil improves. As we wait for the trees to mature and bear fruit, nuts, and fodder, we are investigating and planning small-scale mixed-farming techniques that will include trees, vegetables, poultry, and livestock.

A concern for the world protein deficit, and the marine biological training of John Todd and Bill McLarney, not to mention Bill McLarney's maniacal passion for fish, determined that we should work in aquaculture. As with agriculture, our guidelines were minimal environmental disruption and as little incorporation of machinery or nonrenewable energy as possible. We wanted to develop fish-rearing techniques that would be economical and also workable for those not trained in biology. It was, in fact, the need to maintain warm temperatures in the fish ponds that led to the building of the first bioshelter dome. Our goal was to avoid feeding the fish food such as grains or soy or fish meal that could otherwise go directly to people. The diet of tilapia, the fish that we have worked most with, is largely made up of algae, supplemented with garden scraps, insects, worms, and midge larvae. In trying to minimize the energy consumption of the aquaculture, we sought out methods by which organisms could do work that is now normally done with machines. By passing the water from the ponds through earth and plant filters and over a bed of quahog shells, which house a bacterial population capable of transforming the toxic nitrogenous wastes from the fish into less toxic nitrites and nitrates, which, in turn, enhance the algal bloom, the water is purified without recourse to an expensive filtration system.

Plants and animals to replace machinery; information in lieu of hardware—these ideas, though hardly new, at first seemed wildly radical, like a revelation. We find them increasingly compelling. They have been the mainstay of human survival until the last four hundred or so years.

Our work in aquaculture has included the cage culture

of fish in open ponds, research into alternatives to commercial fish foods, and the work in solar-algae ponds that is described below. In the area of energy, although it is hard to make arbitrary separations of the research into single categories of food, energy, and shelter as the work with them becomes increasingly interrelated, it should be noted that we have harnessed wind energy in several ways. We have used windmills to circulate water in aquaculture systems, to pump water and compressed air, and to generate electricity. The incorporation of solar heat into the bioshelters for space heating and to fire biological systems is obvious. The need to extend the growing season for both fish and plants led to the adoption of a structure that would trap and conserve heat. As we mentioned earlier, the dome was the first such structure that we tried. Although its heating capabilities were most satisfactory, it had the flaws that most domes share. Its ability to conserve heat is less than optimal, and, as is almost invariable, it leaked, leading to Bill McLarney's homily that "Domes belong over fish ponds." Our dome still finds useful seasonal employment as a fish hatchery and a greenhouse, but for a solar structure that remains functional throughout the year, we have looked to other designs.

Following the dome experiment, in collaboration with Ole Hammarlund and David Bergmark of Solsearch Architects in Cambridge, Massachusetts, we designed a small solar greenhouse and aquaculture unit that was the prototype for the Arks on Cape Cod and Prince Edward Island. Originally and rather ignominiously called "the Six Pack," this small greenhouse is almost entirely closed and protected to the north, while a great deal of effort is made to capture incoming light and heat from the south, maximized by painting the interior walls white for reflection. The Six Pack has withstood three winters, two of them unusually severe, without the need to burn any fossil fuel, gracing us all the while with greens, herbs, and hardy vegetables. In addition, it manages to produce early strawberries and thousands of seedlings for the garden. It is proving itself well suited to the needs of a family or a unit of several people. The greatest potential for such a structure would lie in attaching it to the southern end of a house or other building that would benefit from a mutual climatic exchange. In terms of productivity it is also practicable as a separate entity.

From the Six Pack, we proceeded to the design and building of the Arks.

Both Arks have more than fulfilled our early expectations in terms of climate control and productivity. The yields from our gardens and from our fish ponds, one of which has netted harvests ten times greater per unit volume than any other known standing body of water, have far outstripped our projections. Because of this, we feel that there really are workable ecological alternatives to industrial technology, and that should we choose to follow them, there is a sustainable future within our reach.

We realize that not everyone shares our hopeful hypothesis, that the mainstream of society hurtles along its road of ever-spiraling growth, using up dwindling supplies of fossil fuels, largely uninterested, even unaware of our ideas. Much more disturbing, however, and even more threatening to our survival is the development of nuclear technology and the proliferation of nuclear power. As Margaret Mead observed when she saw Goddard College's Vermont landscape sprouting with windmills, solar buildings, and labor-intensive gardens, "it won't mean a thing if we don't stop nuclear power." As usual, she was absolutely right. Our work at New Alchemy with our fish and plants and friendly buildings will amount to little more than an esoteric exercise if that issue is not confronted and ultimately resolved. We are acutely conscious of our debt to the people who have dedicated themselves to educating and organizing the opposition to nuclear power. We further recognize that if we succeed in stopping the use of a form of energy so unforgiving that it is predicated on both human and technological infallibility and leaves a legacy of deadly wastes that will be radioactive for 250,000 years, this is merely the first step in laying the foundations for a future that has the smallest degree of certainty. Nuclear disarmament remains the ultimate objective for planetary survival.

There is a group of men and women who live at Montague Farm near Amherst in Massachusetts who embody the convergent threads of this complex and crucial dilemma. Living on the farm, they are closer to the sources of their own livelihood and have some measure of self-reliance. At the same time, their overall consumption is reduced, lessening the drain that they would otherwise be imposing on finite planetary resources. Their activities range from farming, to community, to holistic health and healing; yet these same people are also leaders in the antinuclear movement. Beyond the obvious value inherent in their work, their example is instructive because they have achieved a combination of the living practice of an ecological ethic and political activism.

The part that we at New Alchemy have played has been to enlarge and make workable some of the options on which a brighter future can be predicated. Our favorite terms for describing the technology that we are developing are nonviolent and restorative. Both convey a sense of interaction between living entities and a recognition that in supporting our own lives some disruption of the world around us is inevitable. It remains an animate world and as such not impervious to our machinations. A nonviolent technology implies some sensitivity to the organic integrity of the living world and is guided accordingly, attempting to recognize and facilitate what mythologists, poets, and mystics have always tried to tell us of the sacredness of life.

We are at this time urgently in need of rethinking the structure of society. We must reexamine its underpinnings of science and technology and the runaway control they exercise over our lives. We have created a science of ecology, but to date we have no understanding of the ecology of science. Such a reevaluation will take time, but certain guiding principles for a new paradigm are becoming discernible. Fundamental to its development is the recognition of the duality implicit in our present understanding. Our thinking has placed us as though apart from other life on the earth. We view the world as other, as outside ourselves, and this is what determines so much of our behavior. We must learn to envision, or rather to re-envision, ourselves as an organic continuum in time and in space with all life and to integrate this consciousness into our relations with all beings. A nonviolent technology is a tool that holds this promise. As the ecologist Paul Shepard once wrote: "Affirmation of its own organic essence will be the ultimate test of the human mind."

PART II

The Evolution of a Theory of Design

There is a fundamental difference between the structure of society and that of the living world. Each subunit in an interlinked global system, whether it is an agricultural or manufacturing unit or a transport system, is incomplete. It cannot function alone. In the living world each subcomponent, while being interdependent, is at the same time a complete unit, whole and autonomous. In this way, two opposite tendencies are fused by nature. For example, a cell is capable of carrying out all the functions normally attributed to life, and as such is a mirror image or reflection of higher levels of organization. It predicts the organism of which it is a component. And while the organism of which it is a part is dependent upon nutrients, energy, and support from other organisms, it is at the same time capable of functioning as a complete entity. In nature a continuity exists in which the smallest living element is an image of each level of organization. A unicellular organism is structured and operates in much the same way as a complex organism such as a tree or a higher animal, which, in turn, has much in common with the ecosystems that sustain organisms. The same kinds of processes and principles of design extend from the organelle to the biosphere.

In the living world, evolutionary design, for some unexplained reason, is continuous and highly adaptive. Inherent in its adaptability may be some of the clues essential to attempting a synthesis of modern knowledge. Such continuous adaptability is very important. It is at once architecture and structure; it is also a dynamic process, developing unity where chaos would otherwise ensue. The First Law of Thermodynamics says that energy is neither created nor destroyed. The Second Law of Thermodynamics says that energy can only be degraded or dispersed. This is entropy, or a measure of disorder. Because no transformation is 100 percent efficient, there is a continuous degradation of the quality of energy. But in the universe and in living forms, rather than degradation into chaos, through the process of entropy we have the creation of spatial forms and morphic order. This may well be energy's last hurrah. Physics versus biology; energy versus life.

Such must be the basis not only for a reintegration of modern knowledge, but for the maps or models we devise for restructuring the ways in which human communities are sustained. Should we uncover the morphic form of the earth and of life within it so that we understand its organization and self-tending abilities, the keys to design will be attainable. The term *morphic* is borrowed from Lancelot Law Whyte,[1] who used it to describe all processes that generate spatial form. He used *morphic,* a word derived from Greek, as a modern name for the spatial expression of the tendency toward unity, order, and intelligibility. This tendency in nature had been recognized as long ago as Plato, but there has been no theory fully explaining it. After 150 years of intensive biological study, however, there are the rudimentary beginnings of a satisfying explanation of how the world works. Some grasp of the adaptive strategies that enable nature to accomplish so much with so little becomes possible. In the term *nature* we mean to include its ecology, successional changes and pathways, and, in a larger time frame, its evolutionary course.

Organismic and holistic biology is perhaps one of the least appreciated and least taught areas in science. Yet in this century an enormous increase has taken place in our understanding of the fluxes, movement of energy, and the physical dynamics of living systems. It is beginning to be understood how living systems reorganize themselves, becoming higher expressions of the possibilities inherent in life. By "higher" we mean simply that which is attainable by the interaction of life forms. Ecosystems change with time. These changes are limited by a variety of factors, including climate, the availability of nutrients, and the nature of neighboring ecosystems. Ecosystems shift from entities that, for example, have initially linear food chains to weblike ones that operate at many levels simultaneously. They tend to accumulate organic matter and increasingly reuse and recycle resources. They tend to become more diverse yet more equitable in the sense that individual elements dominate less. For example, where we live on Cape Cod, as a sand dune gradually becomes a pitch-pine and oak forest, the stratification and spatial structure of the area changes from being rather loosely to more highly organized. The nature of resident organisms changes with succession, and the cycling within becomes increasingly close, having been fairly open in earlier stages. The exchange rates between various organisms and their environment become slower, more subtly pulsing, and wastes or organic matter are increasingly used within the system itself. As an ecosystem evolves toward a higher state, there is an initial selection for rapid growth, a pioneering phase. The ecologist's term is r-selection. As the ecosystem matures, more feedback control is introduced and more elements are integrated into the larger whole. This is termed K-selection. In terms of productivity there is a shift from an emphasis on quantity in earlier successional stages toward one of quality. In the living world, homeostasis increases over time. Symbiosis, the conservation of resources, and, in some cases, the ability to resist perturbations from outside increase. Further information accumulates. Information might be considered to represent the transformation of energy to its most usable state—the last hurrah of which we spoke.

This general overview describes the process by which nature changes over time. Such occurrences as fires and flooding or changes in climate can reverse this process. It is not linear. But nature is constantly organizing, even under stress. Life has adopted a variety of approaches to accomplish given ends. One of the ironies of human history is that most civilizations from the ancient hydraulic ones of the great river valleys through colonial cultures to modern industrial societies have based their support on practices antithetic to the course of nature. All of them have violated principles that, although not yet fully understood, have proved extraordinarily successful for all other forms of life. Civilization has not yet considered devising a culture that emulates the processes of nature. We should like to propose that culture can be transformed through such an emulation.

The fundamental first step is a comprehension of the structure of the complex systems upon which societies depend. We are learning that the structure of a system and not its coefficients determine its ultimate behavior.[2-6] By structure we mean the fundamental mode of organization of a system. Structure is the morphology or basic design that creates the patterns of operation. Just as the skeleton shapes the morphology of the human, modern industrial societies have structural components around which they are organized. Roadways and their transport vehicles represent a major structural element.

By coefficients we mean that which is not itself structural per se but which unites with a structural element to produce an effect. Coefficients are parameters or constants for given elements under a set of circumstances. In the above example, the roadways, vehicles, and the petroleum-energy dependency of the system are structural, whereas the size or efficiency of the internal-combustion engines and the amount of petroleum required to run them represent coefficients. Put in another way, the first set of underlying elements is intrinsic, whereas the second set affects the timetable of events. Structure is what Willis Harman has called the dominant paradigm. Despite its dominance, it is hard to see as one is in it and part of it, which makes it even harder to describe. It may even be that "clarity" or "understanding" usually comes to humans when they think about coefficients. The dominant paradigm tends to create the opposite effect in people, namely a sort of addiction to what exists and a tendency to patch up problems with coefficient-related behavior. This point should become clearer through what follows.

The discovery that structure determines the behavior of a system, if true, will have an enormous impact on all levels of design. It implies that the behavior and fate of a system are determined by its organization and structure, and not by its rate of expression or its coefficients.

The structure of modern industrial Western civilizations and, to a large degree, that of all societies has been fundamentally and radically transformed since the Industrial Revolution. The present structure was predicated on the fragmenting of function. Manufacturing, commerce, and agriculture became separated in both space and time, and there was a division of the city from the countryside. Superimposed on this was a global support network of resources, such as minerals, fibers, and, in more recent times, food. In a period of a few centuries the Western world passed from a condition of somewhat autonomous subunits that were relatively integrated and internally self-regulating to partial units operating in a global context. Originally this was based on imperialism and colonialism and more recently upon multinational economic units. A dramatic change in the energy infused into these systems caused a radical transformation. Energy in one form or another was conceived as being cheap and limitless, either as the coolie or the slave in the colony or as massive quantities of coal. The dependence on petroleum and its derivatives in the last hundred years is an even more dramatic example.

The structure of the contemporary world assumes a foundation of limitless supplies of cheap petroleum. This assumption underlies fossil-fuel-fired generating plants attached to central power networks, and industrial agriculture, which uses between five and twenty calories of petroleum-derived energy to put one calorie of food on the American table. Architecture is comparable in its practices, with massive use of glass, air conditioning, and heating. Transport networks and manufacturing, sustained by fuel-demanding engines, are highly energy-inefficient. Commerce pays little attention to energetics, as the World Trade Center in New York attests. Even medicine is not immune. Industrial civilizations were based upon substances thought to be limitless and inexpensive, which are now known to be finite and increasingly costly.

Structure determines fate. Coefficients vary rates and relative dominances within a system. The physicist Amory Lovins[7] has suggested that if structure and not system coefficients determines behavior, as he believes, our present civilization is fated and will prove unsustainable.

Unfortunately, at the same time that structure is beginning to be seen as pivotal, science and technology are addressing themselves almost exclusively to coefficients. For example, in the transport sector, automobile engines are being designed for greater efficiency. The goal is to double gas mileage over that of a few years ago. This is a coefficient-related activity on the part of technologists. At no point is the transport structure itself, including the highway system and the fuel base, being seriously questioned. Because we have built a society to which this structure is essential, and because, as we know, it will collapse without the automobile, the larger question of transport remains taboo for scientists and designers. The same holds true in architecture. Although architects are devising ways of conserving energy, little attention is being paid to the function of buildings in society. We use separate buildings for teaching, commerce, manufacturing, and living. Food is grown in separate greenhouse structures. The functions of buildings have been separated into distinct units that are incomplete from an energy and social perspective.

Architecture addresses itself to coefficients; structure is left intact. Combining the various functions through integrative design, which could lead to a vision of buildings as "ecologies," is not being considered. This is true in agriculture and in many other key areas of human endeavor. By focusing on the coefficients, science and technology are buying time for society. The ability of contemporary science to improve technology but not alter the fundamental structural society helps explain the drive to develop nuclear power so that there will be enough power within this century to sustain the existing industrial base. A blind attempt is being made to sustain a system that is unsustainable with its highly centralized, interconnected energy grids and its massive use of energy. Genuine alternatives are not readily conceivable. An alternative, which would require a radical restructuring, could lead to more humanly based techniques and environmentally restorative methods of providing for the needs of people. At the present we are trapped in an intellectual cage, created by our own science. The future is either apocalyptic or materialistically euphoric, à la Herman Kahn.

If it is assumed that coefficients are only buying time, the vital support elements of our society must be totally redesigned. For a transition to take place, the new processes being created must be allowed to coexist within the present structure. A beginning can be made by asking simple, fundamental questions. Only by asking such questions can a societal structure that is truly adaptive be foreseen.

It is perhaps the first time in history that people are being asked to create the landscape of the future. There will be little time for the slow adaptation of techniques that has characterized change in human experience until now. The central task now is to find an adaptive structure in which individual lives have a wide range of opportunities available to them within environmental and social contexts that enhance the whole society. In the first place, it should be a structure in which a majority of people participate in the processes that sustain them; in which part of their time is involved in the production of energy and food, and in tending their shelters and the landscapes that nourish them. New kinds of structure imply unprecedented levels of synthesis, for part of the necessary reintegration of the human experience must be a heightened awareness of the natural order upon which we depend. People and process must become one.

The second aspect in the design of an adaptive human-support system is that scale or size be reduced. Present technological societies operate through technocratic elites. Because of such elites, most people are removed not only from the activities that support them but also from control of political and economic processes. If people lived in smaller systems, their experience would be more direct and political judgment on the part of the majority would become more sensitive. It should be possible to redirect science along participatory lines both in terms of the physical aspects of life and in terms of the body politic.

A third basis for an adaptive society is that human needs be fused with the needs of the biosphere. The biosphere is the vehicle that provides us with the gases we breathe, our foods, and the purification of our wastes. From it come all the materials upon which we depend. Ecosystems far larger, far more complex than ourselves or our societies are essential to us. This needs to be acknowledged in the new synthesis. The highest priority is that these ecosystems be *enhanced* by allowing them to fulfill their maximal biological diversity and structural complexity. Only through working with the biosphere can we help ourselves. This is possible if ecosystem enhancement is a basic premise of design.

The fourth essential part is that inexhaustible energy sources such as the sun, the wind, and biofuels should be the primary inputs within an adaptive framework. Natural systems are predicated on these forces. Human ones ought to be. Each region should develop a structure based on the energy fluxes impinging upon it. If this became the basis for design, more autonomous subunits would evolve. They would be more highly integrated into the larger environment and less vulnerable to disruptions or scarcities. Remaining petroleum would not be burned carelessly but could be used for long-lived materials, special medicines, and the like. If the natural energy falling on a region were made the basis for life support, more subtle, less violent technologies would ensue, which would allow for a degree of human involvement now impossible because of the nature of most of our machines. This is the case with New Alchemy's Arks, which are powered by the sun and the wind. Design within an ecological model gives birth to what are now dimly conceived possibilities.

What is an adaptive structure? It would have to include the above characteristics, but to be successful it must go one step further. We must ask: Are there in the living world equivalent processes that, when subtly adapted to structural and electronic components, can sustain societies, performing the jobs presently done by capital-intensive, energy-consuming, and polluting processes? Can organic, living equivalents to the mechanical and energy-demanding support components be found in nature? At New Alchemy we have been exploring this question for several years, and we are finding such living equivalents. Agriculture and energy can be structured on the models of living systems. To do so, it is necessary to integrate biotic elements with structural, electronic, and appropriate technological components, employing the strategies of nature. There may be an adaptive design unity inherent in nature that can be used for human ends.

In the adaptive model of nature lie design ideas that will enable humans to create societies and cultures as beautiful and as significant as any that have thus far existed. In the simplest terms, we must ask such questions as: Can a plant do for us what a gasoline-powered machine now does? This does not mean we must turn our backs on contemporary science. Rather, science needs redefining and redirecting. It will take many technologies and techniques to explore the living world, in particular modern materials and electronics. Energy and climate research will focus on the sun, the wind, and biofuels; food research will emulate the strategies of ecosystems. (By the term *ecosystem* we mean interconnected, interdependent assemblages of plants, animals, and microbes living together and interacting with nonliving components of which they are a part. Examples are a forest, a field, or a pond. In terms of design shelter, housing and building would integrate energy and food findings with architecture.)

The wonder of a plant lies in the fact that it is. From the point of view of design, a plant is noteworthy because of the way it fits into its larger ecology and has through its morphology and physiology devised methods of trapping and transforming energy, using nutrients, creating foods, and providing structure and shelter for itself so that it can withstand perturbation and change. It symbolizes a triumph in design. Plants do a great deal with very little, and yet they sustain many other forms of life. The biological metaphor or analogue may be the most important guide available. If we created a culture in the image of the biosphere, it would bring about a revolutionary change in the way in which people live on the earth. It would have an impact as great as the introduction of agriculture some 10,000 years ago. Biological consciousness would fundamentally alter our sense of what human communities might be. It would be no less profound than the changes in the sixteenth century that led to the formation of the modern scientific world view. Human consciousness and our place on the planet are being questioned. Research on the atom, the naked gene, and other heedless practices we permit are creating, in their shadow, a new sense of identity and destiny. The Ark on Prince Edward Island and its counterpart on Cape Cod are early attempts by the New Alchemists to explore the landscape of the new synthesis. It is still firmly rooted in the contemporary tradition of which we are a part, but it affirms an almost infinite number of possibilities. Henry Drummond's Law of Laws frames the meaning of the theory of design: "That if Nature be a harmony, there must exist a unity and continuity extending through all realms which for me is the physical, organic, aesthetic and mental."[8]

PART III

An Ark for Prince Edward Island

Bioshelter as Habitat

The biologically sophisticated Ark project makes manifest our interdependence with the natural world, reintegrating us into it and enhancing our sense of wholeness: a special strength of combined innovation in energy and agricultural systems.

—Amory B. Lovins

A Prince Edward Island country road. Sign for the Ark.

Northern societies or those in harsh climates have greater energy needs and dependencies than those with milder climates. In order to achieve present-day standards of living, modern industrial civilizations depend upon global networks requiring disproportionately large amounts of fuels, foods, and shelter. Canada and the United States use more energy per capita than any other nations.[1] A good share of Canada's petroleum is burned in heating buildings.[2]

About 55 percent of the Canadian energy use is in heat, nearly all of it at a relatively low temperature, below 140°C. Space heat (less than 100°C.) accounts for over 58 percent of the total heat budget, with the domestic sector using the great bulk of it. Electricity, the subject of so much debate and the scene for so much capital investment, plays a far less significant role in Canada's energy budget. In 1969 more than half of the total energy was consumed as heat and only 14 percent of the total as electricity.

As electricity, fuel, fertilizer, food, storage, and transport costs rise and their petroleum bases dwindle, nations requiring substantial energy will have to reduce their standards of living, which is precisely what is happening at

Cape Spry, Prince Edward Island. The location of the Ark.

the present. Or they have the possibility of taking a bolder step and redesigning themselves to accomplish much more with less. The Ark on Prince Edward Island attempts to do this. It combines into one solar- and wind-powered structure a household, resident greenhouse, a microfarm (including aquaculture), a vegetable greenhouse and tree nursery components, a small barn shop, a waste-purifying system, and a research laboratory. It is a first attempt to create symbiotic associations out of support functions normally separated in space and time. Unprecedented levels of integration between energy, food, and shelter systems have been attempted. As such, the Ark is a first effort at a new synthesis.

With the Ark we redefined how people live and sustain themselves, by focusing on redesign and restructuring at the smallest functional unit of society: the household. Since housing affects the majority of the population and is the major fuel consumer for space heating, human habitations represent a logical starting point in a critique of society. The Ark project began as a question. It asked if it might be possible to devise a human habitation as a bioshelter. A bioshelter is a structure inspired by biological systems, capable of providing its own energy and climate, trading its own wastes, and growing food for the residents.[3-5] We were interested in carrying the concept one step further and designing a human habitation as a bioshelter with the capacity of a small economic unit, which could pay its way through the sale of its surplus power and produce.

In collaboration with Solsearch Architects, the New Alchemy Institute built the two Arks, one on Cape Cod and one in Maritime Canada. The Ark on Prince Edward

A COMPARISON OF THE ARK WITH ORTHODOX HOUSING

CATEGORY	ARK	ORTHODOX HOUSING
UTILIZES THE SUN	Source of Heating, Climate, Purification, Food Production and Much Interior Light.	Some Interior Light — Often Negative Role Necessitating Air Conditioning
UTILIZES THE WIND	A Source of Electrical Energy from Windmill Wind-Driven Circulation through Composting Toilet.	Only Negatively, Increasing Fuel Demands through Infiltration.
STORES ENERGY	YES — in Three Systems and Growing Areas.	NO.
MICRO-CLIMATOLOGICAL SITING	Integral to Design.	Rare.
WASTE PURIFICATION	YES — Except for Grey Water which is Piped into Leaching Bed.	Wastes Untreated and Discharged to Pollute.
WASTE UTILIZATION	Purified Wastes are Nutrient Sources in Interior Biological Cycles.	NO.
FUEL USE	Wood, a Renewable Source, as Supplemental Heat.	Heavy Use of Gas, Oil or Inefficient Electricity.
ENERGY CONSERVING	YES — Also Uses Energy to Serve Simultaneous Functions.	NO, or Rarely.
ELECTRICITY CONSUMPTION	About same as Orthodox House but Electricity Used for Many Productive and Economic Functions.	Fairly Heavy Consumer.
FOODS	Diverse Foods Cultured Year-Round	Not Within — Often Summer Gardens.

Table 1

A COMPARISON OF THE ARK WITH ORTHODOX HOUSING

CATEGORY	ARK	ORTHODOX HOUSING
AGRICULTURAL CROPS	Vegetables, Flowers and Young Trees	NO.
AQUACULTURAL PRODUCE	Fish for Market.	NO.
ECONOMIC UNIT	YES — Viability to be Determined.	NO — Financial Burden.
OPERATIONAL COST	LOW — Ultimately Exporter or Power.	HIGH — Particularly in Fuels and Electricity.
INITIAL COST	HIGH — Due to Energy and Biological Components — Uses Larger Amounts of Quality Materials.	Moderate.
VULNERABILITY TO INFLATION AND SHORTAGES	SLIGHT.	SEVERE.
IMPROVES CLIMATE AND LOCAL ENVIRONMENT	YES — Locally by Windbreak and More Broadly through Reforestation.	RARELY — Most Intensify Weather.
TEACHES ABOUT THE LARGER WORKINGS OF NATURE	YES.	NO.
INCREASES SELF-SUFFICIENCY	YES.	Rarely.
STIMULATES LOCAL AND REGIONAL SOLUTIONS	Possible.	Unlikely.

Table 1 (cont'd)

Island to be described here differs from the Ark on Cape Cod in that it is a human habitation as well as a microfarm. It has, as well, its own auxiliary power-generating and waste-treatment facilities. In the Prince Edward Island Ark, bioshelter design combines the various support elements into a single structure. The Ark on Cape Cod is exclusively an agricultural bioshelter. The Prince Edward Island structure is much more complex. It has to function in an extreme climate at the eastern end of the province of Prince Edward Island in the Gulf of Saint Lawrence. Its location on Spry Point is surrounded by pack ice during the winter and early spring months. The Cape Cod climate is benign by New England standards. Additional heating, trapping, and storing components were required in the Canadian Ark. In order for it to function as a human habitation, its climatic control needs were greater, and internal waste purification and sewage treatment were required. From a design point of view, the Ark on Prince Edward Island is an extension of the concepts developed in the Cape Cod Ark. But because it is more complex in a biosocial sense, there is within it a higher degree of integration. It is technologically as well as biologically more sophisticated than the smaller, less costly Cape Cod Ark.

A bioshelter that is a human habitation is not just a house, although superficially it may look quite similar. From the north side, the Ark on Prince Edward Island resembles an architecturally conservative house that is made more modest by the presence of the earthen berm that partially hides its bulk. But the differences between the Ark and an orthodox house are many and fundamental; the Ark is a microcosm designed to serve a range of human needs not now provided by housing. It is modeled on an ecosystem. Its architecture is solar. In many respects,

Wagon in foreground and newly planted orchard in background surrounding the Ark.

the Ark is the antithesis of the contemporary house. Instead of continuously and wastefully consuming finite substances such as petroleum and other fuels, it attains its climate from renewable energy sources, namely the wind and the sun. A comparison of the Ark with orthodox housing is made in Table 1. From a design point of view, the differences are radical.

The table lists twenty categories or attributes of design. Economics and costs are considered as well as the social and the environmental impact of the two approaches to design. Table 1 attempts to put the design theory into concrete form. The existing structure of housing and housing networks, with sewage systems that dump human wastes into lakes and rivers, and inefficient heating with finite substances such as natural gas that require extensive distribution networks, can be compared with a bioshelter, which is a whole, semiautonomous entity. Several important differences between houses and the Ark should be touched on. The contemporary house is wasteful of the heat it consumes, while the Ark stores heat, including summer heat, at various temperatures and in different ways for use in several climatic and biological roles. Instead of drawing continuously on external electrical and other energy sources, the Ark will cogenerate power with the island utility. An experimental wind-driven power station adapted simultaneously to the needs of the Ark and the requirements of the local utility network has been developed so that power can be produced both for the province and for the Ark. The Ark can accept power from the island utility when the wind is not blowing and return it to the network when it is blowing hard. The New Alchemy research windmill, known as Hydrowind, is hydraulic.*

Because most houses pollute not only through the burning of fossil fuels but also through the discharge of sewage, the bioshelter wastes are treated internally in a dry toilet-composting system. After being purified, wastes are used as nutrient sources in living cycles within. Since the bulk of the heating is solar, emissions from burning are

---

*As of this writing, support for Hydrowind research development has ceased as a result of Canada's deciding to concentrate its windmill research monies on an "in-house" vertical-axis windmill design. Hydrowind, the New Alchemy machine, has successfully demonstrated the value and efficiency of hydraulics for power transfer and electricity generation.

reduced and confined to wood gases from an auxiliary combination fireplace-stove.

Household dwellers normally consume foods that have been stored for long periods, elaborately packaged, highly processed, and transported over long distances, particularly in winter. The Ark produces fresh foods on a year-round basis. While food autonomy is not a design goal for the Ark, a wide array of fresh produce is cultured within, including fish, vegetables, and greens for the

The southern facade of the Ark in winter. Upper vertical area, solar collectors; sloping area, translucent roof.

residents. The residential food-growing area is adjacent to the kitchen. There is an economic dimension to the Ark unknown in contemporary single-family houses or condominiums, which represent major economic burdens. The Ark is designed to produce significant amounts of food, flowers, and young trees. Much of the Ark research has been, and will continue to be, directed toward devising internal food-producing ecosystems that will provide a viable economic base for bioshelter dwellers. Although an Ark is more expensive to build than a conventional house, the fact that it is a combined residence and microfarm with its own internal economy helps it to pay for itself. The processing and sale of crops could underwrite construction, finance, and maintenance costs. This is a design objective, however. It will take a number of years of research to reach it.

There is an urgent need, especially in northern nations, for a dramatic shift in attitudes toward human habitations. In many ways the suburban house represents a failure of design. The designers Day Chahroudi and Sean Wellesley-Miller have summed up the design failure.

Historically, the various utility systems and services that go to make up a home have been developed in a piecemeal manner in isolation from each other. Consequently, while some components or subsystems may be near optimum, the total system is seriously sub-optimal. This state of affairs was relatively unimportant, at least in the short term, during the historical period when the ability of the natural environment to process wastes and supply cheap energy and water was well in excess of the short-term demands placed upon it. Now that we are approaching foreseeable limits, this is no longer the case and something more than a piecemeal approach is called for.[6]

The west-facing end of the Ark, with bedrooms behind balcony,
overlooking the sea a few hundred feet away.

Efforts to apply ecological strategies in the design of the Ark have led to a number of biotechnical breakthroughs. An example of the benefits of a structural shift to a new design paradigm is that the Ark is not only a house. It is, among other things, a fish farm. The fish-culture system is not only for rearing thousands of fish for market but also provides some of the Ark's climatic needs.

The aquaculture facility was designed as both a low-temperature (30–35° C.), solar-powered heat collector and a fish-culture complex. Two rows of thirty solar-algae

The northern facade of the Ark, sunk down behind a wind-deflecting earthen berm.

ponds linked together within the Ark. Light enters the building through the translucent south roof and wall, exposing the ponds to solar radiation. The aquaculture ponds have highly translucent walls and contain dense blooms of light-energy-absorbing algae. The algae not only provide feedstock for the fish but act as efficient solar-collector surfaces. The water-filled ponds perform as heat-storage units. Unprecedented levels of biological productivity have been reached in the solar-algae ponds.[7,8] Fish production per unit volume of water is the highest recorded for a standing water body. This is not the sole function of the aquaculture facility. When temperatures drop in the large greenhouse area and in adjacent rooms, including the laboratory, heat is radiated from the ponds and the building is warmed. In a three-day blackout during a violent, late-November storm, the solar-algae pond complex was the only operational heating system. Temperatures outside dropped below −5° C. and winds were in excess of 50 km/hr, yet the crops within survived.

The design of the solar-heated aquaculture facility was the result of our deliberate search for processes in nature that when combined with appropriate technologies would substitute for fuel-consuming, capital-intensive hardware. In this case, living organisms and a renewable form of energy were asked to replace some of the functions of machines. For example, light was substituted for a range of energy-consuming and expensive equipment normally used for biological regeneration and circulation in the aquaculture ponds. The ponds are made with walls that allow over 90 percent* of the light to enter through the

---

*The Kalwall Corporation of Manchester, New Hampshire, published figures and not readings made within the ponds.

sides. Their placement in the structure where they can best receive solar energy, and the introduction of microscopic algae that absorb the incoming energy, purify the water of fish toxins, and provide feedstocks for fish, result in a new and ecological approach to fish culture and climate regulation. The bulk of machinery, energy demands, and external fish feeds are eliminated. Light, algae, herbivorous fish, translucent building materials, and a cylindrical and modular design allowed such a substitution. The integration of heating and food production freed us from dependence on technologically complex solar heating, which involves collectors containing expensive copper, selective black absorber surfaces, pumps, piping, and heat exchangers. Fossil-fuel-burning furnaces are not used in the facility.

Symbiotic relationships at various levels of design are sought actively. Again, the example of the aquaculture facility in the Ark is fitting. In addition to nurturing a commercial fish crop and heating the greenhouse, it is a source of irrigation and fertilization for the vegetable, fruit, and tree seedlings within. Metabolic by-products and organic matter from the ponds can increase shallow-rooted leafy-crop yields up to 120 percent.[9] The process of creating new linkages between ecological and engineered elements is ongoing and may be increasingly mediated by sensors and electronics devised for this purpose. In one experiment we are coupling fish-raising with leafy-crop hydroponics on the pond surfaces. In this experiment the rigid insulating pond tops are replaced with a floating raft of Styrofoam, which provides support for leafy crops such as lettuce. Lettuce is a moisture-loving crop. Its roots must be in an oxygen-rich milieu for rapid growth.[10] In the experimental system the lettuce roots are immersed in the warmed water. Warmed water that maintains a fairly stable temperature increases lettuce growth considerably. The plants derive most of their nutritional needs directly from by-products continuously produced by the aquaculture and carbon dioxide. The oxygen critical for the roots also comes from the pond, having been generated photosynthetically by the algae in a daily rhythm that may match the oscillating requirements of the lettuce.

In Table 2, the biological-structural approach to design in the Ark's fish facility is compared with the most advanced engineered-technological closed-system aquacultures. The fundamental shift in design toward a new structure can be visualized through this comparison. In the Ark an ecosystem powered by light effectively replaces one engineered for raising fish in small spaces. It is more comprehensive in that it provides climate and resources for terrestrial agriculture within. Biological strategies become a genuine alternative in food, energy, and shelter design. Although Table 2 is confined to aquatic systems, it conveys the scope of the new synthesis as well.

The biological metaphor inherent in the shape, heating, or food-raising aspects of the Ark is valid. The end points of the design process meet basic human needs. In this context, structure is redefined and moved towards culturally adaptive ends.

We have dealt with the new bioarchitectural design ideas at the point of interaction of aquaculture and energy within the Ark. Many other aspects of its design are ecologically inspired. Some of the characteristics the Ark shares with ecosystems are:

1. *Integration.* Energy, nutrient, structural, and biotic components interact through a range of pathways to create a unique environment. An attempt has been made

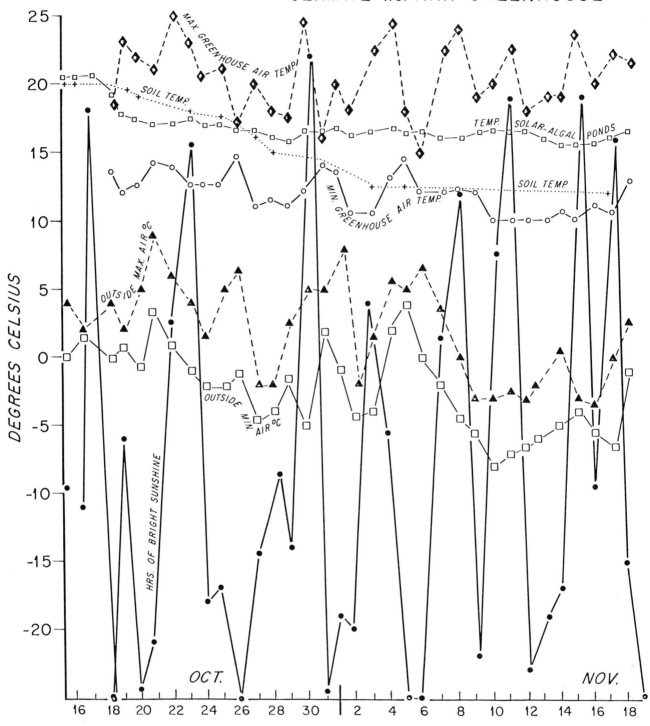

CLIMATE v.s. ARK GREENHOUSE

DEGREES CELSIUS

MAX GREENHOUSE AIR TEMP.

SOIL TEMP.

TEMP. SOLAR-ALGAL PONDS

MIN. GREENHOUSE AIR TEMP.

SOIL TEMP.

OUTSIDE MAX. AIR °C

HRS. OF BRIGHT SUNSHINE

OUTSIDE MIN. AIR °C

OCT.

NOV.

16 18 20 22 24 26 28 30 2 4 6 8 10 12 14 16 18

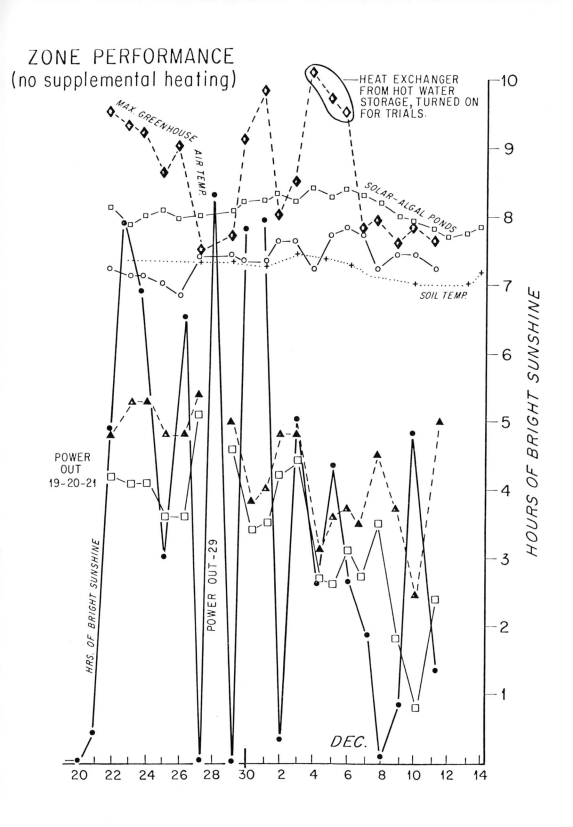

ZONE PERFORMANCE
(no supplemental heating)

MAX. GREENHOUSE AIR TEMP.

HEAT EXCHANGER FROM HOT WATER STORAGE, TURNED ON FOR TRIALS.

SOLAR-ALGAL PONDS

SOIL TEMP.

POWER OUT 19-20-21

HRS. OF BRIGHT SUNSHINE

POWER OUT-29

DEC.

HOURS OF BRIGHT SUNSHINE

20 22 24 26 28 30 2 4 6 8 10 12 14

to achieve relative stability, sharing of limited resources, and high efficiencies within each subelement. The illustration of the residential area shows how closely the various components are tied together in an architectural context (diagram on page 108). The residential food garden is on the left. The hot-water storage, which contains 20,000 U.S. gallons in three adjacent chambers, the solar heating controls, and the composting chamber of the composting dry toilet are in the basement. Immediately above the hot-water-storage chambers are the living-dining areas and the bedroom areas are directly overhead.

The integration between structural, heating, and biotic elements are depicted further in the diagram on page 109. Below the barn-food-preservation area is the 118-cubic-yard rock-hot-air-storage chamber for the 2,000-square-foot (185.8-m²) greenhouse section. Immediately in front is the 20,000-U.S.-gallon aquaculture facility. Under the translucent 2,500-square-foot (232.3-m²) south roof are areas used for vegetable and flower crops. The bench against the south wall is for the rooting and propagating of young trees using mist irrigation. Table 3 gives the square footages for the subelements within the structure.

2. *Redundancy and Diversity.* The Ark's climate is achieved through nine diverse, complementary techniques. It relies upon two active solar hot-water systems, including a 700-square-foot (≈65-m²) collector for space heating, and a passive warm-water aquaculture facility for the bulk of its heating. An active warm-air and hot-rock-storage heating system, in which a fan circulates the air in and out of storage, utilizes solar heat trapped by the building beneath its translucent south face. A heat exchanger transfers energy from the hot-water to the hot-air

system, providing a relatively sophisticated degree of redundancy and control. A wood-fired furnace, yet to be
used, has been installed as an emergency backup system.

Energy needs have been minimized through a number
of conservation techniques. These include few north-side
windows, tight construction methods, and elaborate insu-
lation of up to twelve inches of fiberglass on the ceiling.
The overall energy budget is further reduced through
attention to microclimatological possibilities. Windbreaks
help protect the Ark on all sides but the north. Here an
earthen berm was constructed to deflect north winds over
the building.

The whole system approach to climate control has
already proved its worth. During the same November
storm mentioned earlier, the Ark's windmill was shut
down and Island Utility electrical power was off for three
days. The building was without both its hot-air and its
fan-coil hot-water heating, and the standby wood furnace
was not used because the resident was hospitalized with a
back injury. The solar-algae ponds provided most of the
heat, releasing an estimated million Btu's to maintain a
safe internal climate in the food-growing area despite
subzero conditions outdoors. The illustration on pages
74–75 shows the building's performance during that period.

3. *Renewable Energy Sources.* The Ark emulates nature by
depending upon the effective utilization of solar energy
and its derivatives. The dominant input is the sun. Winds
provide some of the electrical power. Wood is used for
supplemental heat. Biotic components provide gas exchange, humidity regulation, air purification, and waste
treatment, absorb solar energy, and produce foods in
commercial quantities. The diversity of renewable energy

Biologically Designed Versus

	New Alchemy solar-algae multispecies fish culture	Salmonid culture in recycling silo system
Category	Biological-structural	Engineered-technological
Energy source	The sun	Electricity
Energy use	Minimal—radiant. Solar energy, plus supplemental compressed air.	Heavy electrical demand for recirculating, heating, cooling, purifying, etc.
Design emphasis	a. Passive—few moving parts. b. Internal, self-regulating and purifying ecosystems powered by a renewable energy source—THE SUN. c. Internal photosynthetically based.	a. Hardware-based. b. Energy-intensive with rapid flowthrough. c. External foods. d. Emphasis on technological regulation. e. Elimination of plants, animals, other than cultured species. f. Sterilization.
Materials	a. Light-transmitting .060-in. thick fiberglass cylinders. b. Placement in light-reflecting courtyards or walls. c. Auxiliary compressed air equipment.	a. Metal tanks, pumps, filters, water exchangers, heating-cooling units, sterilizers, automatic feeders, cleaners, back-flushing plumbing, columnar gas exchangers, etc.
Structure	SIMPLE—based on maximization of light absorption.	COMPLEX—technologically.
Biotic environments	Relatively complex—photosynthetically based ecosystems.	Simple—elimination of most organisms except for microorganisms in bacterial filters used in water treatment.
Control	Primarily ecological and internal through interactions of microorganisms, phytoplankton, zooplankton, detritus, also through use of several fish species occupying individual niches—occasional water change and sediment siphoning.	Electrical, chemical, and mechanical controls superimposed onto the water body in which fishes are housed.
Likelihood of contaminating fish flesh with poisons	Slight—fish feed predominantly low on food chain, particularly algae in a protected environment. Dangerous chemicals NOT USED for disease control and environmental management—less dependent upon contaminated commercial feeds. Solar-algae ponds do, however, require thorough initial leaching.	Highly likely—fish fed exclusively upon commercial feed, contaminated with agricultural poisons; also these feeds include fish meal from marine species which might contain poisons—toxic contamination from disease and sterilizing chemicals, including algicides, and from stabilizers, etc., in pumps, plastics, piping, etc.
Recirculation	Occasional—low-flow, air-lift pumps used to exchange water between two solar-algae ponds.	Continuous and rapid—up to 1,500 liters per minute (23,760 gallons per hour in a 4,888-gallon facility).
thermal regulation	a. Ponds are efficient year-round solar heaters—algae absorb solar energy thereby heating water. Summer venting and partial shading with plants prevents overheating. b. Heat-tolerant species.	a. Refrigeration and heavy energy requirement for heating to maintain narrow thermal range throughout year. b. Heat-sensitive species.
Oxygen for life support	Generated internally by algae during photosynthesis, supplemented at night with compressed air.	Continuously supplied from industrial oxygen cylinders.
Fish species	Phytoplankton feeding—tilapia and Chinese carps Detritus and zooplankton feeding—crayfish, bullheads, and Israeli carps. All excellent-lasting fish.	Carnivores—trout and salmon—could also be used for raising channel catfish.
Primary feeds	Internally grown feeds—particularly attached and planktonic algae, also zooplankton. Bulk of feeds grown with fishes in the solar-algae ponds.	Processed commercial feeds—prepared from fish meal, soy and grain meals, vitamins, minerals, stabilizers, etc. Most potential feeds also for direct human consumption.
Supplemental feeds	Flowers, weeds, vetch, midges, earthworms. Commercial fish feeds are used in moderate amounts to optimize growth.	Often animal by-products prepared from slaughterhouse offal.

Table 2

Engineered Closed-System Aquacultures

Category	New Alchemy solar-algae multispecies fish culture	Salmonid culture in recycling silo system
	Biological-structural	Engineered-technological
Disease control	Control through emphasis upon disease-resistant species, such as tilapia and bullheads. Mass mortalities from disease rare.	Salmonids sensitive to diseases. Control through H_2O sterilization, chemical and antibiotic treatments, and quarantine procedures. Mass mortalities from disease common.
Biopurification	Toxins purified internally, as algae and other organisms rapidly utilize them as nutrient sources.	Toxins purified through technological steps and tertiary water treatment, including bacterial filtration.
a. Clarification	None—particulates important component of internal ecosystem.	Screening and steam-cleaning to remove particulates.
b. Sulfide toxicity	Not yet experienced.	Occurs when filters clog—requires back-flushing to eliminate anaerobic layers in filters.
c. Nitrite toxicity	Not yet observed—algae photosynthesis prevents nitrite buildup.	Occurs on occasion—water change most effective treatment.
d. Ammonia toxicity	Ammonia utilized by ecosystem. Green algae take up ammonium directly during photosynthesis. Nitrification takes place naturally in shallow sediments. If ammonia should ever build up, tilapia carps and bullheads can withstand ammonia levels up to ten times greater than those lethal to salmonids.	Ammonia toxicity major threat to system. Nitrification through chemical, physical and biological methods. Plastic media trickle filters and/or submerged aerobic bionitrification filters are used. Filter bacteria often preactivated on synthetic growing media.
e. Nitrate toxicity	Toxic levels not yet observed, as most nitrogen incorporated by algae prior to nitrate stage in nitrification process.	Columnar denitrification requiring introduction of outside chemical sources of organic carbon, such as glucose and methanol—column filled with polypropylene flexi-rings.
Holding capacity	Densities of 3 fish/gallon have been held for up to six months—fish ranged from fingerling size to 250 grams.	Salmon smolt densities of 8-10 fish/gallon with continuous dilution of fresh well water at 5-10' rate.
Productivity	Projected fish production of 30-40 kg/m³ per year. First trials yielded 2.55 kg/m³ in 100 days (9.31 kg/m³ per year). Equivalent to approximately 143,000 kg/hectare per year.	Projected fish production of 54 kg/m³ per year, or 1,000 kilograms of 0.5-kilogram salmon in an 18,500-liter system with flow rates up to 1,500 liters/minute. Average flow—620 liters/minute.
Life span	Pond material life span—20-30 years.	Not known. Continual replacement of filters, pumps, subunits, etc.
Management	Amenable to amateurs familiar with aquarium techniques. Novices start with low densities.	Requiring engineering, therapeutic, and handling skills of high order.
Tolerant of mistakes	Tolerant, except for too-heavy supplemental feeding.	Intolerant.
Environmental impact	Beneficial—pond water and by-products used to irrigate and fertilize gardens and orchards.	Varying from little impact to potentially harmful with discharge of treatment chemicals and back-flushed filter materials.
Cost	Capital cost of 25-35 cents/gallon to build depending on light-reflecting courtyard for pond, and aeration system. Facilities with additional ponds will cost proportionately less.	Capital cost of scaled-up 2nd- and 3rd-generation facilities, each with an estimated capacity of 500,000 pounds of fish per year is expected to be 1 million dollars.† Estimated to be equivalent to 80 cents/gallon capacity. Smaller systems much more costly per gallon.
Running costs	Low	High

*Description of ''Technology of Closed System Culture of Salmonids,'' based on 1974 report of Thomas L. Meade, College of Resource Development, University of Rhode Island.
†Personal communication with design engineer, 1977.

Table 2 (cont'd)

networks enables it to function as a semiautonomous bioshelter.

4. *Photosynthetically Based Food Chains.* As in a pond, field, or forest, photosynthesis in the Ark provides the basis for its food chains. In the aquaculture facility, several species of green algae proliferate, providing feedstocks for fish and regulating the metabolism of the fish-culture ponds. (See Table 2 for details.) The growing of food and tree crops is a direct photosynthetic process.

5. *Microbial Pathways for Self-regulation.* Waste is decomposed using microbial means. Human sewage, kitchen, and garden wastes are composted and sterilized biologically.

The Swedish composting dry toilet reduces water use by approximately 10,000 gallons per person per year. Since wastes, apart from gray water, are treated internally, no sewage is dumped into the sea, nor does the Ark require a central sewage-treatment plant. Such a structure situated in a densely populated urban area would save society an estimated $40,000 through internal waste treatment.[11]

The dry toilet–compost system eliminates sewage sludge, which is a major environmental pollutant, and produces instead a high-quality fertilizer that is free of human pathogens.[12] The Ark will produce an estimated 550 to 600 pounds of high-quality fertilizer per year, containing approximately 46 pounds (20.9 kilograms) of nitrogen, 14½ pounds (6.6 kilograms) of potassium, and 6¼ pounds (2.8 kilograms) of phosphorus from human wastes and kitchen garbage. In addition to the fertilizer from household wastes, greenhouse refuse including weeds, roots, and the outer leaves of the crops, seaweed, fish offal, and miscellaneous organic matter will be generated. After one year, waste material is reduced some 95

A R K   S Q U A R E   F O O T A G E S

	Square Feet	Square Feet
MECHANICAL SPACES		
Equipment Room (Net Floor Area)	253	
Rock Storage Duct Work Space	66.5	
Tanks (Gross Including Walls)	441	
Tanks (Net Capacity):		
Tank A	49	
Tank B	113	
Tank C	201	
Total Tanks		363 square feet ≈ 2540 c
Rock Storage Area:		
Gross	480	
Net Usable	400	
Well Room:		
Gross	70	
Net	50	
GROSS AREA DEVOTED TO HEAT STORAGE		921
NET AREA OF TANKS AND ROCKS		763
NET FLOOR AREA DEVOTED TO MECHANICAL		370
COMMERCIAL GREENHOUSE		
Gross Area		1910
Net Usable:		
Fish Tanks	680	
Growing Beds	480	
Suspended Planters*	272	
Circulation	408	
FAMILY GREENHOUSE		
Gross Area		234
Net:		
Suspended Planters and Herb Planter	128	
Fish Tank Area	19	
Circulation	80.5	
ATTIC SPACES		400
WORKSHOP		293

Table 3

	Square Feet	Square Feet
BARN/GARAGE		
Net Interior:		
Floor Level	430	
Loft	200	
Total		630
RESIDENTIAL CIRCULATION		
Net Interior Rooms:		
Entry	80	
First Floor Hall		
(Including Closet)	55	
Hall to Livingroom and		
Lavatory	32	
Upper Hall	40	
Stairs and Landings	146	
Total		353
SERVICE SPACES		
Net Interior:		
Lavatory	27.5	
Bath (Including Linen		
Closet)	47.5	
Laundry	17.5	
Kitchen (Plus Broom		
Closet)	145.0	(54 square foot counter to
Total		237.5
LIVING SPACES		
Net Interior:		
Laboratory (Plus Balcony		
and Closet)	235	
Livingroom/Dining Room	505	
Small Bedroom (Including		
Closet and Shelf)	170	
Large Bedroom (Including		
Shelf, Closet and Loft)	286	
Master Bedroom (Including		
Closet)	207	
Total		1403
OUTDOOR SPACES		
Lower Deck	225	
Upper Deck	72	
Total		297

Table 3 *(cont'd)*

	Square Feet	Square Feet
GROSS RESIDENTIAL		
(Less Family Greenhouse)		1812
GROSS FAMILY GREENHOUSE		234
Residence Total		2046
GROSS COMMERCIAL GREENHOUSE AND WORK-SHOP AREA		2210
GROSS ANCILLARY SPACES		
Laboratory and Balcony	242	
Entry and Hall	140	
Barn and Loft	572	
Basement	350	
Total		1304
TOTAL GROSS BUILT AREA TO BE OCCUPIED		
(Doesn't Include Attics, Tanks and Rock Storage)		5560
GRAND ENCLOSED TOTAL		
(Includes Attics, Tanks and Rock Storage)		6881

Table 3 *(cont'd)*

percent by volume and is completely composted and safe for use as a fertilizer.

The dry toilet is a Swedish Clivus Multrum. It is technologically simple, but in order to function, it contains a biologically complex ecosystem that is based upon chemosynthetic autotrophs. These organisms do not require light to reduce carbon dioxide and to synthesize nutritive substances. A few instructions are all that is required to operate dry toilets despite their biological complexity.[13]

Microbial pathways are critical in other components within the Ark. The metabolic waste products of the fish are treated in the sediment layers of the solar-algae ponds. They are eventually siphoned into the deep garden beds, where they are used as fertilizer. Diverse microbial communities have been introduced into the greenhouse soils to help check plant diseases and pests and to increase carbon-dioxide production. Low levels of carbon dioxide would otherwise limit greenhouse crop production.

6. *Overall Homeostasis.* Homeostasis is accomplished by different routes. Several of these have been described. Our design objective has been to achieve a high degree of homeostasis or control within the Ark with a minimum of energy and cost. Much has yet to be learned, as this is an area in architecture that has been little explored. We have made an effort to create biologically, architecturally, and electronically a number of internal symbiotic elements. Symbiosis characterizes stable and energy-efficient living systems. By coupling food production to internal purification cycles, nutrients are conserved and continuously recycled. We chose to assemble deep and diverse soil ecosystems for the Ark. We wanted soils that would be productive for commercial crops, fertile, and intrinsically

capable of regulating disease and pest organisms. Our "homeostatic" approach to terrestrial greenhouse gardening is not common. It differs from commercial greenhouse practices in that the latter incorporate sterile growing mixtures in shallow benches or growing beds as a substrate for crop culture, which are heavily fertilized and frequently sprayed, fumigated, and sterilized. In the Ark, we sought to create soils that were semipermanent and would continue to increase in fertility over time.

A greenhouse glazing (Rohaglass SDP16—a new acrylic double-glazing) was used that permits ultraviolet wavelengths to penetrate and strike soil and plant surfaces, helping to regulate bacterial and fungal populations and possibly reduce the probability of plant diseases. There were a number of reasons for opting for a deep-soil ecosystem instead of sterilized, chemically managed, shallow growing beds. In the first place, the former does not require biocides, which threaten fish life. Secondly, sterilization is an energy-intensive process requiring heat or toxic fumigants such as methyl bromide or chloropicrin, whereas viable soils are ecosystems capable of utilizing available energy and are highly efficient in energy use. Thirdly, a rich soil environment can generate the high levels of carbon dioxide necessary for optimal plant production. These high levels are often supplied industrially in many commercial greenhouses that are otherwise incapable of supplying their own carbon dioxide needs. Fourthly, weeds and crop by-products, if not sprayed, can be fed to the fishes. Over the next few years it is our intention to compare the biological approach employed in the Ark's contained environments with standard greenhouse practices. For the past two winters, lettuce,

Interior living area of the Ark. Kitchen counter at the far left.

The northern end of the Ark's living room. Under the oak floor is the 20,000-gallon hot-water storage area.

kale, spinach, chard, broccoli, parsley, bean, herb, and flower crops have grown well, being free of disease and relatively unaffected by pests.

The Ark's climatic stability or resistance to external perturbations seems to be remarkably high for a northern climate solar facility that is situated in a region of sporadic sunlight. With its large solar facade, the structure oscillates thermally more than a thermostatically regulated building heated with fossil fuels, but as Figure 1 shows, the environment within remains stable with outside temperatures as much as 34.5° C. colder than inside the greenhouse area. After November 5, the minimum interior air temperature varied only 5° C., the pond temperatures 3.5° C.,

The kitchen herb garden in winter.

88   TOMORROW IS OUR PERMANENT ADDRESS

and soil temperatures 2.5° C. The following winter, the full heat-storage capacity was more fully utilized and thermal oscillations were dampened and the Ark's thermal stability enhanced.

In common with natural ecosystems, the Ark has high levels of internal information and low entropy. It is a miniature world. Its information tends to be organized, internal, and complete, rather than spread loosely among interconnected elements, as occurs in highly stressed environments or in relatively wasteful industrial societies. The comparatively low levels of entropy within the bioshelter enable it to make a more positive contribution than an

The dining area. Agriculturists Wayne Van Toever (far right) and Linda Gilchisan (second from right).

The Ark's residential food- and flower-growing area. The door leads into the production/research component.

ordinary household to the exterior environment or to society. We are attempting to study homeostasis, information, and energetics within the Ark. The laboratory contains instruments and a small computer where thirty-three climatological, biological, and performance characteristics are monitored. It is hoped that through measurement, analysis, and computer modeling using "real-time" information, the broader question of design can be extended.

7. *Interphasing with Adjacent Ecosystems.* Designers tend to neglect creative interphasing with adjacent ecosystems. It should be possible for a household or a building to contribute to its surrounding environment.[14] Most reduce neighboring ecological integrity, and pollute. Ecosystems tend to interact with each other in more subtle and beneficial ways, which include ameliorating and stabilizing climates, and exchanging nutrients and organisms. The Ark minimizes the release of toxic materials from a human habitation. It contains a tree-propagating facility that is intended to help reforest the surrounding region. Mist propagators assist in germinating seedlings and in propagating rooting cuttings of thousands of valuable trees. Most will be fruit, nut, and fodder trees destined for orchards, windbreaks, and ecologically derived agricultural forests. The tree facility epitomizes the ideal that bioshelters not be retreats from the larger world but building blocks for a society rooted in the concept of stewardship.

Living and working in a structure where the sun, the wind, architecture, and ecosystems are operating in concert can be an extraordinary experience. It seems to foretell what the future could bring. Each of us involved in the project would like to live one day in an Ark-inspired

Production/research area: seedlings being propagated under mist. The sea can be glimpsed through the left window.

bioshelter. Its psychological impact is not easily described. The Ark, as a humanly derived microcosm, creates a sense of wholeness and integrity engendered by a high degree of self-sufficiency. The growing areas function as halfway stations between the residential interior and the external environment. There are no barriers, only external "membranes" separating inner living and laboratory spaces from the biological working areas and the out-of-doors. There is a natural progression from one subenvironment to another. Because of this, the world outside is less alien and even an ally as the source of one's fuel and power needs.

Working with vegetable crops, flowers, or trees, or tending the fish while a howling blizzard rages is exciting. Watching the sensors in the laboratory read out the Ark's various functions and monitor its health while the cold wind rages connects one consciously to the forces sustaining all life. One feels immediately useful, knowing that tree seedlings will help in reforesting and that the crops will help to feed the community. Knowing it is a center for gathering knowledge leads to a sense that untold possibilities exist and that the dialogue has begun. It is our feeling that bioshelters can extend the human experience in northern climates.

The adoption of biological models for design should have immediate and widespread application. Material and fuel scarcities and increased pollution will necessitate that society shift to more semiclosed systems for performing crucial tasks. But the shift could take place within the old paradigm rather than through a new synthesis. It is not given that design approaches borrowed from nature will be adopted. It will probably not be understood that there is a need to rely upon organisms organized into ecosystems in order to continue vital functions of society. A totally engineered approach overlooks the necessity of a partnership with nature. It assumes erroneously that strictly physical and chemical technologies can cope without massive and cheap fuel subsidies. Only living systems can do this. The recent debate over U.S. plans for the colonization of space has exposed the fallacy of relying on completely engineered life-support systems for long periods of time.[15,16] Nor is an all-technological solution elegant. It has a tendency to be bulky and to use too many materials. It is neither reproductive nor self-maintaining, and if all its

Lettuce intensive-production bed at the Ark. Toothed-shaped bars are part of the vent-opening mechanism.

Ark computer/monitoring specialist Al Doolittle standing behind a young fig tree.

A mixed planting (foreground) including a eucalyptus, which comprises a microcontrol ecosystem for pest regulation, and a lathe area production zone for tomatoes.

structure, functions, and controls are composed of metallic hardware engineering, it will be poor at energy utilization.[17] A greater potential lies in the ecological design and engineering of complex ecosystems. These have the advantages of self-maintenance, respiration, and controls, partly in the form of multiple species of organisms that allow for natural combinations of circuits and "biohardware" selected probably at thermodynamic limits for power and miniaturization for millions of years.

The Ark is one of the first synthetically framed explorations of a new direction for human habitations. With its use of diverse biotic elements, energy sources impinging upon or generated at the site, and internal integration of human-support components normally exterior to households, it begins to redefine how people might live. The Ark is not an end point, but an early investigation of a new direction. As such, it gives concrete form to conserver society concepts.

We are using the Ark to explore other designs and applications in various regions. Most recently it has been used as the informational basis for designing villages which are solar ecologies. A computer-based system records and stores this information, which is used for modeling and simulations.

Computer models using the experience of the Ark will rapidly improve the design of bioshelters. The Ark is unusual in the sense that it can be monitored as a "complete" system containing biotic and engineered elements. It can also be divided into subcomponents to elucidate couplings and dependencies. The monitoring already has defined the Ark as a dynamic system of interacting components. This growing body of information can be used to

The two avenues of linked solar-algae ponds used for trout and tilapia culture and for solar heat storage.

Close-up of solar-algae ponds for raising trout. Note rafts containing comfrey being grown hydroponically on the pond surface.

The solar-algae ponds are connected to form a recirculating river. Part of the recirculating water is purified by passing through a vermiculite bed containing tomatoes and comfrey. The agricultural crops help clean up pond water.

develop computer models of the Ark's dynamic systems. The models can be verified accurately by comparing their predictions to the subsequent behavior of the Ark. Once the model is proved realistic and accurate, it can be extended to model hypothetical bioshelters of differing design in environments unlike that of Prince Edward Island.

Such uses of simulation are well known in industry. While they have been attempted for environmental studies and ecosystems, it is rare that the systems under study can be carefully monitored or manipulated. The Ark provides us with a powerful tool for approaching larger theoretical questions of design. The computer techniques applied to design aircraft or chemical plants can be applied within the Ark to explore holistic design theories from an ecological point of view. Ecologists have used systems analysis before but not in the conceptual and useful way that will be possible with the Ark.[18] A mini-computer installed in the structure is used for much of the initial modeling as well as for monitoring and regulating the behavior of the systems. Thus simulation and observation can be done together in "real time."

The application of Arks throughout society seems assured, although the widespread usefulness of bioshelters and bioshelter concepts will be questioned and opposed on a number of social, legal, agricultural, and economic levels. One senior agriculturalist has criticized the concept on the grounds that North Americans are demanding increasingly that their food be prepacked, predigested, prepared, and ready to heat and serve. Bioshelters producing fresh food run counter to current trends. His statement is contradicted by food sales; despite rising food costs, Canada imports fresh produce from Florida, California,

Another type of aquaculture filter at the Ark. Here the water passes on its return journey through pipes in which tomatoes are growing. It works!

and Mexico, and still sustains a $15 million annual greenhouse food crop in the face of rising fuel costs and inefficiently designed structures.

As well, there is a small but growing number of people wanting high-quality fresh-grown foods. Another sector, one that often overlaps with the prior group, wants to know the source of their foods and to be assured that they are grown in relatively biocide-free environments. They will pay a premium for such foods. On Prince Edward Island, where food tastes are not generally sophisticated, the demand for produce from the Ark has outstripped our supplies. Even if the Ark were altered from an experimental to a production facility, we could not meet the demand in the rural area where the Institute is situated. In other words, a large number of bioshelters producing year-round foods would have ready access to local outlets because such markets are not easily saturated.

The full value of bioshelters for northern societies will not be realized until power and fuel costs increase further and shortages and disruptions of fuel supplies take place, as has been the case with natural gas in many parts of the United States. Compared with poorly built and poorly insulated oil- or gas-heated houses, the higher initial capital costs of bioshelters may limit their adoption for a number of years. This period should allow for the design and testing of second- and third-generation structures, with increasing emphasis on sophistication of design and minimization of costs. We are beginning to foresee a potent new direction for bioshelter development, where passive heating-architectural components and ecological entities play an even greater role than in the present New Alchemy Arks.

Possibly the most serious criticism of bioshelters is that they are too complex. Being engineered ecosystems containing high levels of information, they are esoteric, beyond the average person's ability to operate and maintain. While it is true that the Ark is the product of a synthesis

New Alchemy's hydraulic wind-driven power plant Hydrowind at the Ark. N.A.I. windmill research and development head Joe Seale is tuning the machine during trials.

created by biological designers, materials experts, agriculturalists, a soil specialist, an integrated-pest-control scientist, algologists, fishery experts and fish culturalists, architects, solar-energy scientists, electronic and computer designers, a systems ecologist, a philosopher, and aeronautical and hydraulic engineers, the overall design objective was to fabricate a system with its accompanying controls that could be taught to and even improved upon by nonspecialists. There has been a conscious effort to design the Ark for lay people.

New Alchemist Ron Zweig describes part of this process in chronicling a small food-growing bioshelter built over four years ago. Just prior to the quote, he has described the sensor-monitoring instruments he devised.

Through the use of information gained with this instrumentation, it will be possible to describe how such a microenvironment could be maintained optimally with much simpler recording devices. We shall be able eventually to compile a list of parameters which can be monitored chiefly through human observation. This could be done with humidity, temperature, sight, smell, etc. If, for instance, a pond began to have an odd smell, one would know that a portion of the water should be changed with fresh or that the flow through the filtering system should be increased. A color change, from green to brownish hue, would evoke a similar reaction. High temperatures of humidity could require venting the inside atmosphere with the outside cooler, drier air. An overcast day would indicate a decrease in the amount to be fed to the fish to allow for the low oxygen or toxic waste metabolism; i.e., ammonia, by the phytoplankton. Many biological factors in the area of our work have been well documented. We are discovering others that we shall have to incorporate in a simple guide to managing these systems. This addition of instrumentation to our work allows us to redefine our bioshelter research and optimize productivity through integrating basic biological principles and the information gained in our observations of their interactions.[19]

Through sophisticated and sensitive instrumentation we are searching for signposts and keys to enable future tenders of bioshelters to do without expensive mechanical and electrical controls.

A complementary approach is being followed by Albert Doolittle, monitoring-computer specialist for the Ark. He is devising tiny microcomputers to match precisely the needs of the Ark's subsystems. Their capacity and programming will be simplified, and the cost of their fabrication will ultimately be much less than most microprocessors available today. His work will interphase human, biological, and electronic controls, so that a relatively inexperienced bioshelter resident could be trained by the systems themselves without having to worry that his or her inexperience might lead to failure in any major subcomponent. For example, on an overcast day, the microprocessor, basing its decision on accumulated information and incoming sensory inputs, might print out or display instructions telling the resident to cut back 50 percent on supplementary feeding to the fish. It would further explain that the low light had reduced the ability of the algae to produce enough oxygen to cope with the biological oxygen demand that would be created by normal levels of supplemental feeding. Under other circumstances it might request reduced feeding because of an unexplainable

The Hydrowind power plant on the ground. Note the hydraulic
pressure gauges on the right and the 10 kw generator on the left.

buildup of ammonia. Based on "real-time" information, it could go on to suggest diagnostic procedures.

In our specialist society we tend to underrate the capabilities of a majority of people. There is a deep human tendency to seek a dialogue with nonhuman organisms. While it often appears in an atrophied form in pet owners,

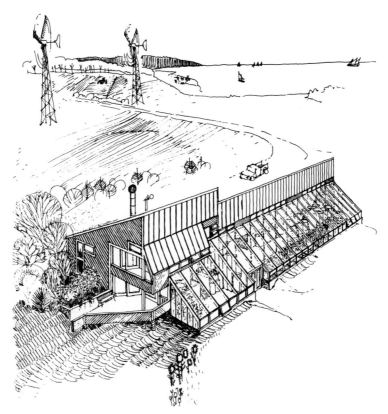

Cape Spry, and the southern aspect of the Ark.

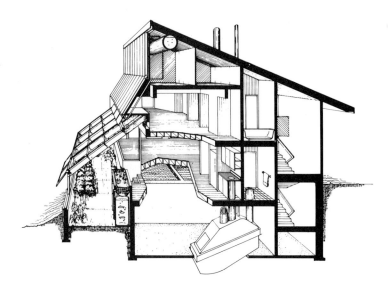

Cross section of the Ark through the residential greenhouse, the kitchen, and upstairs bedrooms. Note hot-water storage area in the basement, the domestic hot-water storage in the attic, and the composting toilet in the lower foreground.

for example, the tendency is almost universal. Plant-filled windows of high-rise apartments attest to this. Although feeding a dog from a can or watering a plant is hardly tending a complex ecosystem, there are people who maintain vegetable gardens or tropical fish aquaria, and in so doing are, in a simplified form, caring for ecosystems. The step from a garden or aquarium to a bioshelter is one of

Cross section through the Ark's aquaculture and agricultural zones. The large rock-heat storage area is shown on the bottom left. Hot air is ducted through central pipes from greenhouse to the rocks. Two avenues of solar-algae ponds are depicted in the middle and the agricultural area on the right. Above the rock storage is a shop. The loft is now offices.

degree, not kind. In 1978 over half of the householders in North America had some kind of food garden. There are many million tropical-fish hobbyists. Both these facts suggest that people are willing to work with ecologies based on the same principles as exist within the Ark. These people represent a broad cross section of society.

There is yet another way of looking at our contention

that the prerequisites for bioshelter living exist widely in our culture. A few generations ago, the majority of North Americans lived directly off the land. Although sound stewardship was not a characteristic common to these rural agriculturists, most of them had enough biological savvy to operate highly diversified family farms and homesteads and to build the culture we have inherited. Most people knew how to sustain themselves. If the need or desire were broadly felt, in a few years enough modern ecological, engineering, electronic, and agricultural knowledge to manage a bioshelter could be taught. The Ark for Prince Edward Island is the first test of these assumptions.

PART IV

The Cape Cod Ark

An Agricultural Bioshelter

Part of the southern facade of the Cape Cod Ark on a winter day. The Pinson windmill is in the background.

The Ark at the New Alchemy center on Cape Cod is smaller and less imposing than the one on Prince Edward Island. Before the solar courtyards were added, it had a rather shiplike quality, reminiscent of a sailboat come to anchor in a field. Perhaps this is because, with the earth piled high on the north side, leaving only the roof visible, the material most in evidence is the translucent fiberglass used for passive solar collection. It is milky-white and is shaped into a series of concave scallops that form much of the roof and most of the southern wall in one long-angled slope, so that from a distance the effect is not unlike that of sails aslant in a wind. Although it does not closely resemble any other structure, it is not jarring, as so many innovative buildings are. It gives one a friendly feeling, both outside and inside.

The solar courtyards added two walls, also scalloped, like wings of white concrete, to the east and west. The walls act as reflectors, maximizing the light reaching the solar-algae fish tanks that are placed in front of them. The entire ground area in front of the building is covered with white marble chips (at the suggestion of the former astronaut Rusty Schweikart), again to take every possible

The entranceway after a winter storm. The solar-algae ponds can be seen just through the windows on the left.

advantage of light for both plants and fish. On a sunny day, there is a powerful white brightness, reminiscent of the whitewashed houses and streets of Mediterranean villages. One journalist has described the Ark as being like a spaceship. This is more than a little contrived. There are people who think that the future and space are synonymous. In its rooflines, the Ark has remained fairly close to Cape Cod tradition. And the molded white concrete of the reflector walls is much more like elements of Algerian architecture and definitely not a substance suited for launching into space. In many ways, the form of the Ark is eclectic, borrowing from some traditions and pioneering in others, but in scale, and even more in the life it contains, it is not unfamiliar and forbidding, but rather welcoming, and to many people, exciting.

This Ark was also a collaborative design effort between Solsearch Architects and the New Alchemy Institute. The sun provides all of the heating. In 1978 a stand-by stove was removed after the bioshelter had thrived for two relatively harsh New England winters. The heat is stored predominantly in the translucent aquaculture ponds, although there is a 43-cubic-yard rock-storage-hot-air system for short-term heat storage and thermal regulation. The interior aquaculture facility, consisting of nine solar-algae ponds, is in the west end of the Ark. There are five additional ponds in the central agricultural zone.

Next to the aquaculture room is the rock-storage area. In front of it there is a 2,872-gallon (10,870-liter) sunken fish-culturing pond that is also a source of nutrient-enriched irrigation water. The area on top of the rock storage is designated for experimental vine crops, and behind it is a microcomputer, encased in humidity-controlled glass-fronted housing. And above it all, just under the roof, suspended from the vault of the structure, is a small platform laboratory.

The central area is agricultural, and is used for evaluating food crops suited to this type of solar climate. It is here that the varietal testing of marketable crops is carried out. This section is terraced into four tiers. Running along the south wall there is a long, low bench on which the mass propagation of tree, flower, and vegetable seedlings is done. In zones that receive limited light, small ecosystems, or biological "islands," have been established as undisturbed habitats for the organisms that we have introduced or encouraged and that pollinate crops and control crop pests. Departing from the orthodox greenhouse practice of sterilizing the soil, deep, enriched, living soils are used as the growing medium for the plants, and for gas production, particularly carbon dioxide, as well. The eastern end of the Ark has a work area and a production bed for vine crops such as tomatoes.

The linkages between the aquaculture and agriculture are many. The fish systems provide irrigation water and nutrients like fish feces and dead algae to the crops. The weeds, cuttings, and other agricultural by-products are in turn often fed to the fish, comfrey being the great favorite.

We intend the Ark to be considered as a prototype microfarm, differing from existing greenhouse facilities in many fundamental ways. These include: (1) solar heating rather than the conventional fossil-fuel heating, which accounts for more than 50 percent of the costs of raising food in greenhouses in cold climates; (2) heat storage, which utilizes the fish-culture facilities and, as well, a rock-filled subterranean chamber; (3) the use of warmed, nutrient-laden aquaculture water for irrigation and fertilization, largely eliminating the need for commercial fertilizers; (4) the use of terrestrial plant wastes as feed for fishes and at the same time the indigenous culture of feedstocks for the fishes in the form of algae and zooplankton; (5) the use of algae-filled solar tanks or ponds as solar heat collectors as well as fish-culture components; (6) the integration of aquaculture with greenhouse plant-raising components, in the aquaculture using Chinese polyculture strategies, and in the terrestrial system's ecological, multistory design; (7) the control of pests by biological methods through the introduction of lizards and insects that are predatory on various pest species; (8) an emphasis on investigating species and varieties of food plants adapted to the natural climatic variations within the structure, as an alternative to energy-expensive climatic manipulation, goal-oriented to a specific or specialized product; (9) the planned incorporation of an integral, windmill-powered, freezing and food-storage plant; and (10) the utilizing of the insulated north walls, roof, and reflective interior walls

A section of the Ark's west end solar courtyard with solar-algae ponds. Despite snowy weather, the pond water, heated by the sun, remains warm.

to reradiate light from the sun and the southern sky onto the growing area in order to conserve heat losses and to maximize the light available for plants.

The Ark, as a microfarm, inevitably shares a number of characteristics, such as plant propagation and culture techniques, with orthodox greenhouse and cultivation practices. In both instances, soil moisture is controlled through irrigation and humidity is controlled and air circulated in order to lessen the possibility of plant disease. Disease-resistant varieties of plants are used in conjunction with intensive planting and management techniques. Like commercial greenhouses, we are interested in and working with such crops as tomatoes, cucumbers, and lettuce that have a high market potential.

The two years that we have spent to date on research have begun to validate the concept of a bioshelter. We have achieved ecological stability and disease and pest control without turning to biocides. Both the agricultural and aquacultural environments have proved very productive. The yields from the aquaculture have been excellent, while in the winter, in the greenhouse, we have grown cash crops to maturity. We have identified a number of varieties of food crops adapted to the bioshelter solar environment and initiated a microcontrol ecosystem and a biological management program. So it seems our contained ecological approaches to food culture are proving viable.

Working with so many biological intangibles forced us to make a number of operational assumptions. We postulated that there were nutrient cycles and biological regulation mechanisms in ecological entities that could sustain a productive agriculture. We decided that the subcompo-

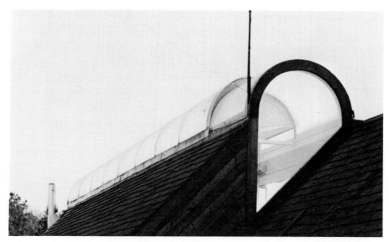

The vaulted vent, partially open to let out excess heat. It is sealed shut from November through March.

The northern aspect of the Cape Cod Ark prior to the installation of the windmill and the planting of the surrounding orchard.

Interior view of east window through a grape plant. The stove on the left has been removed. The building is exclusively solar.

Second and third tiers in the central agricultural zone; during the winter the cement area is the rock storage chamber, and the rectangular area near the vault is its intake. The steps lead to the scientific instruments and a tiny laboratory.

nents for this should come from a variety of wild ecosystems, and that to assemble the appropriate ecological combinations, "seeding" from many different environments would be required. We knew that the information carried by ecosystems far exceeded our knowledge and in the final analysis might prove unknowable, but we did not think that this needed to be a hindrance in design because, with or without our comprehension, ecosystems would continue to perform critical regulatory functions within the bioshelter.

Sterile soils and the use of toxic chemicals are common to food culture in orthodox greenhouses. We opted for deep, biologically diverse soils that we "seeded" from the fields, meadows, and forests in alluvial, limestone, and glacial areas of southern New England. This is an ongoing process. To the soils we added compost, seaweeds (for trace elements and structure), and composted leaf litter. Our intention was that the soils be very fertile, with a high content of organic matter and good water-holding ability. We were designing for pathways within the soil for the multiple exchange and storage of soil nutrients. We wanted carbon dioxide production to be optimized through dense bacterial activities and diverse animal populations that would include earthworms and predators for pest organisms. The overall intention was that the soils would achieve a structural complexity that would lead to the formation of many microhabitats and create a dynamic balance between pest organisms and their control agents. The early evidence is showing that these strategies work. The crops grown in our soils have been healthy and have shown good yields. In the Prince Edward Island Ark, the structure of the soil was such as to enable predatory ladybird beetles (*Hippodamia* sp.) to complete their life cycles in the upper layers. In the Cape Cod Ark, pathogenic fungi, the presence of which had been unknown, attacked the eggs of aphids (*Myzus persicus*) and helped to control them. The use of water has been minimal and the buildup of salts slow and controllable. Although we have yet to verify it, there are indications that the biologically active soils may produce sufficient carbon dioxide to supply the high demands of the crops at noon on sunny days.

Most agricultural environments are intrinsically unstable because the crops are planted, removed, and altered from season to season. This instability can lead to pest outbreaks because biological regulatory mechanisms do not have time to become well established. In the Arks we have increased the ecological diversity and biological stability through the creation of aquatic and terrestrial "islands" throughout the interiors. These "islands" include stable perennial plants such as herbs, flowers, and grasses, like bamboo, that are not cropped. These provide stable habitats for pollinators, predators, and the parasites of pest organisms. Among the predators are wasps, flies, predatory mites, spiders, frogs, and lizards. The aquatic "islands" have a special function in that they offer a habitat for damsel flies that prey on whiteflies (*Trialeurodes vaporium*) and other pests. The entire network of undisturbed islands is located in growing areas that are less than optimal for crop plants. It creates a pleasant aesthetic and functions as a sanctuary for organisms that range over the crops and protect them.

Greenhouse pests have invaded the bioshelter periodically. Our tactic has been to try to control their numbers, rather than to eliminate them. To date, very little economic damage has occurred because the introduced control agents have kept the pests in check. Shortly after the Cape Cod Ark was completed, the greenhouse whitefly (family Aleurodidae) was introduced accidentally on flowers that had been donated to us. We sent for a tropical parasitic wasp, *Encarcia formosa,* to regulate the whiteflies. The measure was effective, and to our surprise and great pleasure *E. formosa* remained in the Ark despite the fact that it reportedly does not survive temperatures below 55°F. In April they resumed parasitizing whitefly scales.

The micro realm of a plant.

In the winter of 1977–1978, aphids or plant lice (family Aphidae) appeared, but by March they were being controlled by a small native wasp, *Aphidius matricariae,* which had entered and established itself in the bioshelter on its own. A parasitic fungi, probably brought in with one of the soil samples, attacked and destroyed aphid eggs during the winter and early spring. In April, syrphid flies (family Syrphidae), which look like bees, appeared, attracted to the flowers. Their larvae preyed upon the aphids and also helped in their control. Ladybird beetles (*Hippodamia* sp.) were introduced intentionally as backup control agents against whiteflies.

The next major pest to appear was the spider mite (*Tetranychus* sp.), which concentrated mainly on the marigolds. Nine hundred Chilean mites (*Thytoseiulus persimilis*) were released into the Ark. Concurrently, a native predatory mite entered the building, and together the exotic and the native began controlling spider mite numbers.

The most recent pest to be observed was the greenhouse thrips (*Heliothrips haemorrhoidalis*), which is of subtropical origin. Initially their numbers climbed alarmingly on several vegetable crops, but for a reason we have yet to discover, the population then declined to acceptable levels.

We have begun to investigate a wide range of crops suited to the environmental conditions which exist in the Ark. The average soil temperatures in the Ark for the coldest months of 1977–1978 at a depth of 2 inches were: November, 60° F.; December, 59.5° F.; January, 55° F.; February, 59° F.; March, 62° F. We grew lettuce, endive, kale, chard, beet, Chinese cabbage, spinach, and parsley varieties for evaluation as to which were best adapted to

A spider's web in this pesticide-free environment acts to trap hundreds of whiteflies, a notorious greenhouse pest. Note the spider on the verge of eating one of the whiteflies.

An ecological cornucopia: lettuce, chard, mustard greens, comfrey, bamboo, banana, New Zealand spinach, Boston ivy, and tropical papaya in the center. Fish-filled solar-algae ponds in the background.

the thermal and light regimes within the structure. Several varieties of lettuce that originated in Holland proved superior to domestic varieties. It is possible that Dutch greenhouse crop-breeding conditions may closely approximate conditions in bioshelter environments in the northeastern United States.

On Cape Cod, during seasons when tomatoes are imported, retail prices can approach and often exceed $1 per pound. This influenced us to establish a production plot in the Ark to study the culture of tomatoes in a bioshelter. On twelve plants in 24 square feet of space during two months of cropping, one variety (tropic tomato) produced 98 pounds. This yield figure is probably low because we know that some of the crop was illicitly harvested by visitors. If half of the internal area were devoted to tomato production, yields for an equivalent length of time could approach 8,000 pounds. From past experience we expect to extend the cropping season into late fall, and to begin again in late winter, spring, and early summer, for a six- to eight-month harvest season. If this is borne out, potential yields from 1,000 square feet of bioshelter space could reach 24,000 to 32,000 pounds annually.

The integrating of the various subcomponents of the Ark and optimizing their relationships is to be a major area of endeavor. Several years ago we discovered that irrigating with aquaculture wastes or pond water increased yields of lettuce by up to 120 percent.[1] The aquaculture wastes were fertilizing as well as irrigating this nutrient-demanding crop. We plan to treat half of the production area with aquaculture wastes and the other half with tap water and compare the yields. It is possible that the by-products of the aquaculture could provide a complete nutrient diet for heavy-feeding tomatoes.

We also intend to experiment with rafting vegetable and flower seedlings on the surfaces of solar-algae ponds. The biological activity of the ponds should provide carbon dioxide, oxygen, warmer temperatures, and nutrients for the plants. Fish excretory products would be the primary source of nutrients. Preliminary tests with comfrey indicate that this type of space-saving method may work when there is a dense population of fishes in the pond. Several species of the fish prefer the partial shade that is created by the rafted plants.

The west end aquaculture room in the Cape Cod Ark. An empty solar-algae pond is balanced between two filled ponds on the lower level.

Because most of our bioshelter work ventures into territory that sometimes involves new materials or new associations of materials with living systems, we are sampling soils, plants, water, animals, and edible portions of foods and testing them for a broad spectrum of toxic materials. These include heavy metals, agricultural poisons that have been or are still in use on Cape Cod, and highly toxic materials such as the pthalmates that are sometimes used in plastic manufacture. Early evidence from tests for lead and cadmium suggests that the Ark functions as a screen and that its soils are less contaminated than those in the external environment.

A jade plant silhouetted against the Ark's translucent southern roof.

The Ark and its whirring windmill at moonrise on a winter day.

Simultaneous with the development of small-scale, decentralized, and sophisticated energy, food, architectural, and manufacturing networks, new economic forms are emerging. It seems very likely that ecology, which is rapidly becoming a major design science, can easily complement economics. Certainly it helped us to outline a possible direction for microfarming.

We feel cautiously optimistic about economic microfarms like the Ark. This is borne out of several breakthroughs we've had at New Alchemy that particularly involve the Cape Cod Ark. The first of these involves our success in the miniaturization of ecological processes, such as the miniaturized terrestrial and aquatic ecosystems in the Ark that have been created without a loss in biological integrity. This is perhaps best illustrated by the solar-algae ponds, which sustain fish populations as dense as 3 per gallon, and also by the intensive indoor gardens that produce crops throughout all seasons without recourse to machinery, chemical applications, or auxiliary fuels. This was accomplished through ecological complexity, space-fitting plant-structural relationships, and the presence of light-reflecting surfaces within the bioshelter.

Secondly, the productivity of the Ark has outstripped our predictions. The yields of 8 pounds/square foot/two months of tomatoes have been described. With better-matched varieties and new designs that will permit us to make use of the upper reaches of the bioshelter, we think that yields will more than double and could possibly treble. The aquaculture in the solar-algae ponds is productive. Yields have been more than an order of magnitude higher than any others recorded for still-water aquaculture, going as high with tilapia as 15 kilograms/tank/year.

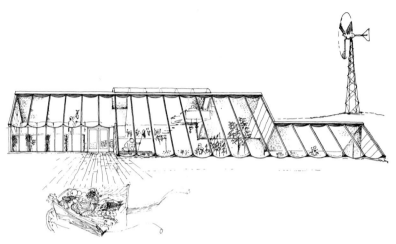

Looking through the southern facade into the interior of the Cape Cod
Ark.

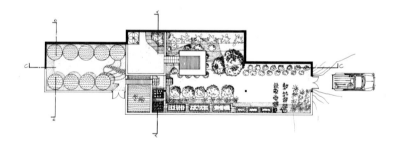

Looking down into the interior. Aquaculture room at left, rock storage
and pond through *A,* and the agricultural zones in remaining area.

THE CAPE COD ARK   133

Another benefit that was not totally foreseen has been the synergistic interaction of the functioning of the systems. The aquaculture serves not only as a food-growing system but also as an effective heat trap and storage medium, at once heating the Ark and producing a crop. Further, it provides fertilizer and nutrients for the agriculture and tree-propagation units.

Lastly, and most happily, the energetics of the Ark have proved satisfactory. The solar-algae ponds pay for themselves in contribution to the climate of the structure alone. An input-to-output analysis yielded a 5:1 positive energy contribution of the aquaculture system. The calculations are as follows:

INDIVIDUAL POND

INPUT	OUTPUT
Capital of Fiberglass[a]	*Heat Stored and Released*[b]
\$75[c] · 1.93×10^5 Btu/\$[d]	2.5° C./day · 2.4×10^6 cm³
.252 cal/Btu · 1/20 yr =	150 heating days/yr =
182×10^6 cal/yr	*900×10^6 cal/yr*

[a] Capital costs are based upon custom fabricating. Bulk or wholesale purchase would reduce the costs.

[b] The output figures are conservative. Since diurnal ranges of 3.9° C. may be closer to daily contribution to climate, then $1,200 \times 10^6$ cal/yr may prove more realistic.

[c] 1967 to 1977 is ten years. Inflation is approximately 1.07–2.0. Thus actual retail 1977 costs were halved.

[d] C. Bullard, *et al.,* Energy Flow Chart Through the U.S. Economy. Center for Advanced Computation, University of Illinois at Urbana, 1975.

The pond system has several advantages over traditional climate regulation in greenhouses that may have an important bearing on the future viability of bioshelters. Not only does output greatly exceed input, but the whole system is independent of fuels, electricity in the heating cycle, and from unpredictable interruptions in supplies. The competitive advantage of such an approach to food production should strengthen over time. The energetics bear up in this area as well.

Comparison between different types of food production can be misleading. For example, there is relatively little fossil fuel used in growing grains, but large amounts are required in the various forms of processing necessary and in cooking. Eggs and fish, which require more calories of energy to produce, can be cooked lightly, thereby becoming energetically competitive with grains.

Rawitscher and Mayer[2] have calculated the number of kilocalories of energy needed to produce 1 gram of protein in U.S. food production before processing or cooking. We have made the same calculations for our fish culture, basing our figure not on projected yields but on yields we have already achieved. Our figures include the capital of the aeration and support components, electricity for aeration (a major contributor that we intend to reduce in subsequent designs), feeds, and labor. Solar-algae pond monocrop aquaculture at New Alchemy requires approximately 100 kilocalories of energy to produce 1 gram of protein.

Bioshelter-based aquaculture is more efficient energetically than most other forms of aquaculture. The following comparison, using the Rawitscher and Mayer figures and more recent data,[3] place our research in a larger perspective.

COMPARISON OF KCALS OF ENERGY TO
PRODUCE 1 GRAM OF PROTEIN

Aquaculture

New Alchemy solar-algae pond aquaculture	= 100—edible portion
Catfish culture U.S.	= (195—edible portion)
Malaysian prawn (Hawaii)	= 328—edible portion
Oysters in raceways in Hawaii	= 400—edible portion

Animal Husbandry

Eggs	= 132
Broilers	= 149
Feed-lot beef	= 800

Grains

Rice	= 40

The comparison shows that solar fish culture at the New Alchemy Institute, although recently developed and not yet refined, is sound energetically. We hope that new designs can again increase both production and efficiency.

Modern agriculture is dependent upon such externals as fertilizers, machinery, and fuels. These have been minimized and internalized to a large degree in the Ark. For example, the aquaculture is based on fish species that feed low on the food chain. The bulk of the food for the fish is produced internally, by the ecosystems themselves. In many cases, it takes less than a pound of dry supplemental feed to produce a pound of fish. Other crops from the Ark provide some of the supplemental feeds.

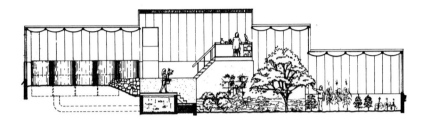

The Cape Cod Ark interior. Note the small laboratory suspended from the ceiling. Aquaculture room on the left and the agricultural zones on the right.

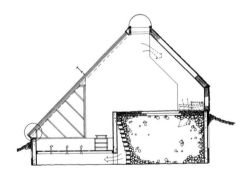

Section AA: Through the rock-storage-hot-air cycle.

The aquaculture is a source of irrigation and nutrients for the agriculture. The humidity that is partially created by the aquaculture provides plant-propagating conditions that are close to ideal.

The Cape Cod Ark cost approximately $35,000 in 1976, including solar courtyard and architecture, but excluding the two computers and sensors. We hope to reduce these costs further. Minimal acreage requirements would allow such a food-growing entity to be situated close to markets. Conceivably, the area required for a microfarm could be confined to an acre or less. The prices commanded by bioshelter foods might well be higher than for most foods, as premium prices will be paid for "organic" food grown in biocide-free environments, especially as the knowledge that environmental carcinogens are the major cause of cancer

Section BB: Through aquaculture room showing the placement of the solar-algae ponds in tiers.

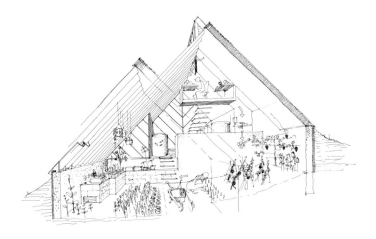

Sketch of interior of Cape Cod Ark through its central agricultural zone.

becomes widespread. Ultimately, the bioshelters may be for post-petroleum-era agriculture what barns were to pre-petroleum farming, essential as ameliorative extenders of seasonal cycles.

PART V

To Begin Again

For people who live in a climate in which they must cope with long months of hard, frozen ground, cold, snow, and ice, having access to a bioshelter can be as revitalizing as the proverbial old-fashioned spring tonic. Once, on a frigid day in February, we took friends to see the Cape Cod Ark for the first time with their children. The sun was bright, glancing off the icy snow, but the wind was biting. We slithered and skidded toward the Ark, clutching the children, the children clutching at us. The rutted ice had nowhere relented into puddles except right in front of the building, where the reflected sunlight in the solar court-yard had forced a slight glacial retreat.

The feeling on opening the door of the Ark and stepping in was one that compares to the moment of stepping out of a plane newly arrived in the tropics, having flown out of winter. At once we were engulfed by moist, soft, warm air and the smells of plants and earth. All of us, even the children, paused for a moment and let it wash over us. The next impression was one of green; of the depth and vibrance of the green of the plants in contrast to the hard, bright, white-and-blue world that we had just closed the door on.

We began to move about and explore, shedding clothes as we went. Down and wool had begun to feel prickly and cumbersome. The children dashed about, discovering frogs and flowers and a strawberry in blossom. We launched into an explanation of the building as our friends drifted about, enjoying first the flowers—nasturtiums, geraniums, alyssum, and the inevitable New Alchemy marigolds—then the range of plants and herbs. Finally we wended our way to the solar-algae ponds, where the children had glued their noses to the outsides of the tank, waiting for a fish to emerge through the gloom of the deep-green, algae-laden water.

It was, granted, one of those propitious, kindly days when the Ark was at its best, well past its solstice slump, with an eighty-degree temperature brought on by the intense sun. But even after many seasons, with the novelty long gone, we find it impossible to be blasé about being close to our bioshelters. The earthy smells and the greenness are wonderfully reassuring. The earth is, after all, only asleep. Winter is not absolute and eternal, however fierce and adamant it seems. And we have a distinct feeling of satisfaction—bordering at times, we're afraid, on smugness—that apart from the fossil fuels used once in manufacture, this climatic outpost of a garden is not based on an ongoing and illicit consumption of a nonrenewable resource. Nor is it robbing other people of their share of that resource. Nor—again except during its manufacture—is it a source of harm to our area of the Cape. And beyond the unquestioned economic and gustatory pleasure, there is an unqualified joy in knowing we can provide our family and occasionally our friends with fresh salad, herbs, and vegetables grown without poisons. Knowing the amount of unavoidable toxicity in the environment has always made us anxious to give our children food that is as untainted as possible. It is a small gesture, but comforting.

Another rather gratifying instance of a bioshelter in action is one that has been built on a homestead farm in rural Nova Scotia, where it was added on as a wing to an old farmhouse. With it, in spite of a very severe climate that has the combined disadvantages of a long, harsh winter and a short growing season, in addition to the stored garden vegetables, there is a possibility of salads and a more varied diet in all seasons. This is worth remarking in that, as in so many remote areas, the produce available from stores is both expensive and usually fairly tired. Fresh salads in winter, an almost Mediterranean wealth of tomatoes and peppers through the hard November frosts, embellish rather than displace northern, traditionally preserved and stored vegetables and fruits. To be poor under such circumstances is not to feel poor. Across the Northumberland Strait from Nova Scotia, the Ark on Prince Edward Island has yielded voluptuous harvests of eggplant that have been somewhat dubiously received by the nonplussed islanders.

The potential and possibilities for adaptations for the bioshelter are many. Many have already taken place. The same architects, Ole Hammarlund and David Bergmark, who worked on our Arks have gone on to design and build several energy-efficient houses in the suburbs of Charlotte-town on Prince Edward Island. They have kept the cost of their houses in the vicinity of $37,000 (in Canadian money), low enough to be of real interest to islanders of average income rather than just a whim of the privileged. The Ark there is pioneering another useful application for the bioshelter. It is being partially utilized as a tree nursery, and as such, as an epicenter for reforestation, in that thousands of tree seedlings will be cultured there. On Cape Cod the various bioshelters already contain thousands of fruit and nut-tree seedlings.

In Manhattan, Ole Hammarlund and David Bergmark have undertaken a project in conjunction with the People's Development Corporation. They plan to include many of the solar-heating, greenhouse, and aquaculture components of the Ark in one of the rehabilitated buildings that PDC is renovating in the East Eleventh Street area. Once it is functional, the people who run the program plan to utilize it as a neighborhood educational facility and to add a store for selling the produce. A similar project is under way in the South Bronx. And in Brooklyn, Solsearch is redesigning an old brownstone for conversion into a bioshelter.

If much of the early work on bioshelters has taken place in the Northeast, it is probably due to the impetus of the climatic goad in combination with fast-rising fuel costs. There are projects in other parts of the country, however. In California, innovative research is being done by Suntek, a research firm that includes Sean Wellesley-Miller and Day Chahroudi, who were among the first people in the field and who coined the term *bioshelter*. Originally from MIT, where they started their work, they are experimenting with substances that will strongly influence the course of bioshelters and of solar architecture generally. They have invented a material known as a heat mirror, which permits light from the sky to penetrate a building but blocks long-wavelength heat from escaping. Another material called "cloud gel" becomes opaque to skylight when the building overheats. They are also working with an effective heat-absorbing and -storing material that they call Thermocrete. All of these substances are now in a testing phase.

Should the idea of the bioshelter catch on and become widespread, the implications are many. Economically, it could provide a decentralized source of produce the year round for a neighborhood, community, or village. The reduction in transport fuels and costs that would result is obvious. There are good prospects for a solar greenhouse business in raising produce, flowers, flats, or house plants, or as a nursery for trees for market. With the renewed popularity of community gardens, a large bioshelter would open the possibility of continuing to garden in all seasons. An artist-therapist friend has suggested the advantages of using the bioshelter as a center that would combine crafts and therapy. She feels the sense that it can provide simultaneously of shelter and of closeness to the earth is soothing, centering, and creative. There are other possibilities on a large scale. Sean Wellesley-Miller and Day Chahroudi suggest that their materials will facilitate a bioshelter approach in apartment buildings, universities, and a variety of public buildings.

Margaret Mead was most encouraging about the ideas perpetuated by biotechnic technology generally and by New Alchemy. She felt that such ideas could provide the structure for a society that could again be reduced to a personalized human or community scale, one in which neighbors and generations would meet and know one another in the daily exchanges of living. She considered this to be a more promising societal framework for the inhibition of aggressive impulses than the industrial, urbanized conditions that so predominate at the present, in which we go nameless, faceless, and unconnected to each other over years and lives. In regard to further research at New Alchemy, she was most concerned that we direct our bioshelter designs away from the single house and toward village and community applications. This was not only because she thought that greater neighborhood exchange would be fostered in this way, but also because she considered that single-family dwellings will be increasingly beyond the means of most of the people of the world. Because of this, the next step at New Alchemy will be toward investigations of the possibilities of ecological village design. This does not, of course, disallow the practicability in terms of both fuel and food costs of a small attached personal or family solar greenhouse.

We are often asked at New Alchemy about the amount and hours of work involved in the maintenance of a bioshelter. This, of course, will range considerably with the individual or people involved, and can be as variable as the number of hours spent on housekeeping or gardening. It is hard for us to make estimates based on our own work because so much of it is in the form of the research activities for a pilot project. Much of the time is spent in monitoring and in collecting and evaluating data. Less esoteric but still within the purview of experimental work are such pursuits as weighing and recording all the produce to determine yields, or counting the numbers of a specific insect to determine predator-prey relations and the efficacy of various methods of biological control. Caring for a bioshelter is little different from including the tending of a garden as a part of one's household, an extension of domestic activities, unless one is operating it as a small business. And the time spent in planting, weeding, or picking can be weighed against the time that would otherwise be needed for shopping and driving. The extra few feet dashed to the greenhouse instead of to the spice rack for a snippet of fresh thyme or dill can, like virtue, be its own reward.

Beyond the concrete advantages implicit in the adoption of the bioshelter on a significant scale, which conservatively could be predicted as being economic, technological, nutritional, and ecological, there is yet another hopeful possibility; that of a perceptual change. One of the countless indictments that can be brought against our current modus operandi is of the buffers and distances that it has put between us and an immediate experience of the natural world. It is not only that we are lessened by this alienation. In being so out of touch, we are cut off from vital feedback from nature. We know, intellectually, that the air and water are contaminated and daily grow more so, but we can filter the air and purify the water and, for the time, protect ourselves and ignore the warning signals. The diversity of the gene pool of the planet diminishes, species vanish forever, but, protected technologically, we still prevail.

Paradoxically, although it is derived from technology, the bioshelter removes the barrier between the human and the other living elements in the system. In the miniaturized biosphere or ecosystem, feedback is immediate and is ignored at the expense of the health of some of its components. Because they are prototypes, in both of the Arks the various systems that comprise the whole are carefully monitored, as we have already described. They are watched over like a hospital patient in an intensive-care unit. This is done because we feel, as innovators, we have an obligation to have as thorough an understanding as possible of the interactions and complexity of the whole and of the sum of its parts. A problem or irregularity shows up very quickly on the instruments, and we are promptly made aware of it. But to be relevant in any broader sense, we think that a bioshelter should be equally workable for people who have no desire to use a computer. We are, in fact, using the data from the Arks to create analogues of sensory signals that will serve as a guide to observing the various systems. Should, for example, the pH of an aquaculture tank begin to rise, or the level of dissolved oxygen reach too low a level, there may be a telltale change in the smell and color of the water, and anyone working near it would be able to detect the problem. This kind of watchfulness is really stewardship on a reduced scale. And the fact that the scale is small should not be seen as qualifying the experience. Working or living in a bioshelter can provide a setting for a renewed intimacy between ourselves and the forces that ultimately sustain us. The exchange of information is prompt and direct. Perhaps it is not too farfetched, assuming a connection, however little understood, between mindscape and landscape, to hope that the learning resulting from such a gradual rapprochement in our relations with the natural world might have wider reverberations.

Even if the healing of the breach between the human and natural worlds will take time, there are more immediate rewards in being involved with a bioshelter. One outcome of caring for living things is often a slow integration of faculties that have long been treated as separate. In contrast to the fragmentation, meaninglessness, monotony, and alienation that characterize so much of modern work, divisions between mind and body, between thinking and doing, become much less apparent, as do the dichotomies of the left and right hemispheres of the brain and those of reason and intuition and of stereotyped sex roles. It is not an unfitting place for mulling over the haunting question posed by Julian Jaynes: "How do these ephemeral existences of our lonely experience fit into the ordered array of nature that somehow surrounds and engulfs this core of knowing?"

Working in a bioshelter makes one aware of the subtle interconnections between apparently disparate elements: between hours of sunlight and plant growth, between relative humidity and the health of the plants. Increasingly, one becomes aware of processes, patterns, and relationships. Whereas science, in the main, has proceeded on a linear, cause-and-effect paradigm, the attempt to work with whole systems begins to undermine the exclusive validity of this approach. We begin to see that we are dealing with a multidimensional web of forces, all of which affect and interact with each other.

In the much broader context of the relation of mind and nature, Gregory Bateson has asked: "What pattern connects the crab to the lobster, and the orchid to the primrose, and all four of them to me? And me to you? And all the six of us to the amoeba in one direction and to the backward schizophrenic in another?" We do not at all wish to imply that we are so much as approaching any answers to such a complex tangle. Yet we do find that in working with biological systems and struggling to become attuned to the dynamic flux, to become increasingly immanental, we are being made aware of the existence of such patterns.

The question of the complex interrelatedness of whole systems is beginning to be applied to global ecology. Two prominent biologists, Dr. Lynn Margulis of Boston University, and Dr. James Lovelock, who is British, have put forth a theory that they are calling the Gaia hypothesis, after the Greek earth goddess. They are entertaining the possibility of viewing the biosphere as being comparable to a single organism, able to control at least the temperature of the earth's surface and the composition of the atmosphere. This led them to the formulation of the proposition that the living matter, the air, the oceans, the land surfaces, are part of a giant system, able to control temperature, the composition of the air and sea, the pH of the soil, and so on, to be optimal for the survival of the biosphere. However, with the exponential increase in human interference in the biosphere, the natural distribution of plants and animals is rapidly being changed, ecological systems are being destroyed, and whole species are being altered or deleted. The danger here lies in the fact that any species or group of species in ecological association may contribute just that response to an external threat needed to maintain stability. This has led them to wonder whether it is possible that, even as our existence is dependent on Gaia, might Gaia also need us in order to continue? Might humanity not provide Gaia with the equivalent of a central nervous system, an awareness of herself? Through us she could have a rudimentary capacity to anticipate and guard against threats to her existence. Then could it be that, in the course of human evolution within Gaia, we have been acquiring the skills necessary to ensure her survival? Such a theory is fraught with evolutionary irony, bearing out well the Taoist point of view. As Stewart Brand once paraphrased Bob Dylan, "In Gaia, we're all 'all tangled up in blue.'"

The hypothesis of Drs. Margulis and Lovelock may or may not be borne out with time. What is pertinent to our subject is the scientific substantiation of the biological metaphor. What has been so strongly intuited by many people is being corroborated and made respectable by science, which we still regard as the arbiter in such matters. Should science incorporate into its ethic the Buddhist respect for all sentient beings and the realization that sacred though the right to truth may be, the search is at too high a cost if it violates a complexity of life that we have yet to understand, then the Gaia hypothesis will have served us well.

The question remains: Even should quite a number of people be persuaded of the wisdom of a renewed bond with the natural world, and of a way of life that does not violate that bond, can they possibly make any difference? It is indeed a quixotic gesture in the face of the entrenched technocratic establishment. Those of us who espouse the cause have long learned to contain simultaneously within ourselves the anomaly of intellectual pessimism and glandular optimism. As to the question of our chances, they are only better than if we try to do nothing at all. As Lewis Mumford concluded *The Pentagon of Power:* "On the terms imposed by technocratic society, there is no hope for mankind [sic] except by 'going with' its plans for accelerated technological progress, even through man's [sic] vital organs will all be cannibalized in order to prolong the megamachine's meaningless existence. But for those of us who have thrown off the myth of the machine, the next move is ours."

It might seem that those of us advocating a different path are open to charges of hubris in challenging so much that seems immovable and irreversible, in maintaining that we have another, even a better way. Our message should not be interpreted as doctrinaire, that we think that only we have seen the light and can unravel the threads of the future. What we are striving for is to keep the options open, to create a structure for what Dennis Meadows, the coauthor of the Club of Rome's "Limits to Growth Study," has called a "sustainable future," one in which our children and their children and grandchildren for countless generations, we hope, will evolve and coevolve in and with the world in ways we cannot foresee.

Seen from the vantage of this much larger perspective, the bioshelter is a tool, a seed, a catalyst in the ongoing flux of time and human and planetary history. We think that it has the potential to be a useful and instructive tool, allowing for intensive cultivation for human sustenance while leaving other areas free as wilderness. It embodies the intention to foster and to nurture life, and to rekindle an awareness of the continuity of the part of humanity within the larger workings of the biosphere. The New Alchemy Arks were created to function as miniaturized ecosystems in which, through the combination of the most advanced electronic sensors and the most ancient sensitivities, we should undertake this search, that looking down from the pinnacle of technological achievement in the late twentieth century, we may review our course and select that which we need to go on. To begin again.

Notes

Part I: The Historical Climate

1. Irene Claremont de Castillejo, *Knowing Woman: A Feminine Psychology* (New York: G. P. Putnam's Sons, 1973).

Part II: The Evolution of a Theory of Design

1. Lancelot Law Whyte, "Towards a Science of Form," *Hudson Review* 23 (1971): 613–632.
2. C. Alexander, *Notes on the Synthesis of Form* (Cambridge, Mass.: Harvard University Press, 1973), p. 216. See especially the Preface to the paperback edition.
3. W. W. Harman, *An Incomplete Guide to the Future* (San Francisco: San Francisco Book Company, 1976), p. 160.
4. H. S. Horn, *The Adaptive Geometry of Trees: Monograph in Population Biology 3* (Princeton: Princeton University Press, 1971), p. 144. Structure in forest ecosystems. See especially Chapter 8.
5. A. B. Lovins, "Scale, Centralization and Electrification in Energy Systems," *Proceedings Oak Ridge Associated Universities Symposium: Symposium on Future Strategies in Energy Development.* In Press. A concise elucidation of the relationship between structure and behavior.
6. D'Arcy Wentworth Thompson, *On Growth and Form* (Cambridge, England: Cambridge University Press, 1959), p. 16.
7. Lovins, "Scale, Centralization and Electrification."
8. Quoted in Whyte, "Towards a Science of Form."

Part III: An Ark for Prince Edward Island

1. F. Paturi, *Nature: Mother of Invention* (New York: Harper & Row, 1976), p. 208.
2. V. R. Puttagunta, *Temperature Distribution of the Energy Consumed as Heat in Canada,* cited in A. B. Lovins, "Exploring Energy-Efficient Futures for Canada," *Conserver Society Notes* 1 (May–June 1976).
3. S. Wellesley-Miller and D. Chahroudi, "Bioshelter," *Architecture Plus* (November–December 1975): 7.
4. D. Chahroudi and S. Wellesley-Miller, "Buildings as Organisms," *Architectural Design* 3 (1975): 157–162.
5. N. Jack Todd, "Bioshelters and Their Implications for Lifestyle," in *Habitat: An International Journal* 2 (1977): 87–100, and in Irene Tinker and Mayra Buvinic, eds., *The Many Facets of Human Settlements: Science and Society* (New York: Pergamon Press, 1977), pp. 87–100.
6. Wellesley-Miller and Chahroudi, "Bioshelter."
7. R. Zweig, "The Solar-Algae Pond Saga," *The Journal of the New Alchemists* 4 (1977): 63–68.

8. J. Todd, *The Ark for Prince Edward Island: A Report to the Federal Government of Canada,* 1977: 79 pp. N.A.I. (P.E.I.) Publication, Souris, Canada.

9. W. O. McLarney, "Irrigation of Garden Vegetables with Fertile Fish Pond Water," *The Journal of the New Alchemists* 2 (1974): 73–76.

10. C. Tudge, "An End to All Soil Problems," *New Scientist* (May 26, 1976): 462. This is an article on the recently developed nutrient film technique, profoundly influencing market gardening.

11. Savings based on 1974 estimate of advanced sewage-treatment facilities and network costs of $4 million for 500 people. Calculation based on five Ark residents. Figures cited in *The Futurist* (December 1974), p. 875.

12. Clivus Multrum, the system used in the Ark, was approved by the National Swedish Board of Health and Welfare after years of testing. Cited in "Toilets That Don't Need Flushing," *Catalyst for Environmental Quality* 1 (1975): 15–18.

13. R. Lindstrom, "A Simple Process for Composting Small Quantities of Community Wastes," *Compost Science* (Spring 1965): 30–32.

14. M. Wells, "Underground Architecture," *Co-Evolution Quarterly* 11 (Fall 1976): 85–93.

15. J. H. Todd, "Biological Limits of Space Colonies," *Co-Evolution Quarterly* 9 (Spring 1976): 20–21.

16. A. Ballester, *et al.,* "Ecological Considerations for Space Colonies," *Co-Evolution Quarterly* 12 (Winter 1977–1978).

17. H. T. Odum, "Limits of Remote Ecosystems Containing Man," *American Biology Teacher* 25 (1963): 429–443.

18. D. Botkin, personal communication.

19. R. Zweig, "The Solar-Algae Pond Saga," *The Journal of the New Alchemists* 4 (1977): 63–68.

Part IV: The Cape Cod Ark

1. W. O. McLarney, *The Journal of the New Alchemists* 2 (1974): 73–76.

2. M. Rawitscher and J. Mayer, *Science* 198 (1977): 261–262.

3. John Bardach, East-West Center, Hawaii. Unpublished data.